'People have told stories for centuries, which keep their hopes and tragedies alive long after those people have passed away. 'Secret Box' is a story about a quest that is exciting, emotional, funny, insightful and at times difficult. Shadows of the past can prevent us from enjoying our lives in the bright sunlight. Here the author shows us the courage needed to make the shadows disappear.'
Tritia Neeb, Consultant in Personal and Team Development, Djihn, Netherlands.

'Philip Larkin may have been right about the impact our parents have on us but, in this compelling and intriguing tale of exploration, the author is determined not to be 'handed on misery' and rather to open hearts and minds, to learn lessons and to hand these on instead. Brave and very personal, not many books make their impact as viscerally as this.'
Gordon Lyle, former People Director, Asda.

'I find myself completely absorbed. It is extremely difficult to put down. There is this sense of courage, and sometimes outrage at the rawness of it, yet I feel deeply privileged to be let in. I was touched through the good things, the utter support, the honest challenge, the genuine caution, the love through the anger. So many parallels. This enables the reader to connect in with themselves in an immensely powerful way.'
Jeremy Keeley, Founder, Sadler Heath.

'It's a page-turner, in parts like a detective novel. It's a story of legacy and transition, and gifted to the children. We observe the relationship between parents and with their children, moving through past, present and future. It is complex with many moving parts. There is the author's voice making sense of things for the reader. It's about how we construct memories and how memory lets us down.'
Mary Joyce, Principal, Leading Minds.

Tony Page is a Chartered Psychologist specialising in organisational development. He coaches leaders and teams in businesses, governments and NGOs in the UK and internationally.

During his career working with senior executives, he has learned effective coaching, facilitation, narrative, theatrical and developmental methods, which are described in Tony's other two books: "Diary of a Change Agent" (1996, Gower) and "Creating Leadership: How to Change Hippos into Gazelles" (2018, BEP).

Tony grew up in Kent, lives in South West London and has travelled widely for work and pleasure. He is married with grown up children, and recently turned sixty. He and his wife Helen spent time last year volunteering in Myanmar and Nepal for VSO.

# Tony Page

## Secret Box

### Searching for Dad in a Century of Self

*Tony Page*

12 March 2018

Telling
Stories

First published 2018 by Telling Stories Press

Disclaimer
This is a work of nonfiction. All the stories in this book are true,
although the names of some people and organisations have been
changed to protect their privacy. The events are portrayed to the best
of the author's understanding. Certain conversations, which cannot
be recalled word for word, and forgotten details have been created
to support the known events. The author accepts that other people
will have a different memory of the events, conversations and actions
described.

Design and typeset by ACE.
Cover design: Philip Mann

ISBN 978-1-9999607-1-1

'What is most personal is most universal.'

Carl R. Rogers


'I recall my father
The one I came after
Who shepherded my laughter
And washed me in the bathtub
Oh when I was a boy
He was devoted to my joy…
… this is how it is again
And this is how it's always been
Now whether we forget
Or whether we keep remembering.'

Nick Mulvey


'The pain we create avoiding pain is avoidable.'

R.D. Laing

# Contents

## DEDICATION

To Auntie M and Uncle D for breaking the silence.
To the child inside each one of us.

# Part One:
## The Plughole of History

## Chapter 1: Extraordinary

Where can I possibly begin?

There was an extraordinary shocking event in August 1969 that hinted at the enormity of our family predicament. After this we managed, and possibly even conspired, to ignore the events that transformed us, and nothing was ever the same.

*'Can you see the other side?'* Dad asks as he gazes southwards across the Deben Estuary towards Felixstowe.

We aren't yet used to his black hair being combed forward instead of the neat parting, and his two days of stubble are the start of a new beard; but there is nothing out of the ordinary about his navy blue holiday shorts and brown leather sandals.

I grunt, my brother nods, and the five of us are silently staring at the tide rushing in, trying to fathom Dad's reason for asking.

*'How long would it take to swim?'*

No one replies although everyone can tell that Dad has ants in his pants, and someone else has to bring the common sense. Mum has taught us that.

We began that morning, Thursday 14th August, waking up under canvas at Hollesley Campsite, and ravenously hungry after a long night of rain. Our trips to the washroom are negotiated clutching toothbrushes and damp, smelly towels, with our wet feet skidding across the sodden grass. The clearing sky and our sausages popping on the Primus stove do little to dispel the grumpiness hanging around us like last night's clouds.

I am fourteen, bored, and longing for adventure. Cold downpours and damp clothing are a price I am willing to pay. During breakfast, Dad's plan reveals how we will escape, and this is appealing, but the chores of washing the plates and tidying the tents sour the mood again.

When we climb joylessly into the turquoise Cortina estate (GGK 845C), I know Dad wants us to be happy, but we can't lighten up because already the day isn't going well.

We are supposed to be going to a beach, but it isn't sunny enough for that to fun.

Lined up on that breezy riverbank, Dad is looking for the ferry that will take us across the River Deben to a sunny beach. There is no ferry to be seen. Mum spots that Dad is about to propose an adventure, and she makes it clear she isn't keen:

*'Please don't endanger us'.*

My ten-year-old brother turns to her: *'I can't swim that far!'* Dad kills the timidity stone dead: *'Nonsense, you're already a strong swimmer!'*

My brother pulls himself taller.

The next thing from Dad is provocative: '*Don't we believe God will protect us?'* Mum hisses back: *'Stop it! Just use your Common Sense. You are being impossible!'*

Dad's religion clashes with Mum's risk assessment. He begins to preach: *'When we take a risk, God is there for us, provided we believe…'.*

Mum is twisting her head rapidly side to side taking in the situation. Her face is contorting in fear then in fury, while her mop of ginger hair is doing its own thing.

Dad presses on regardless: *'… but if we just keep ourselves safe, we will always be afraid. Only when we risk something, will God move to protect us'.*

He speaks about God, but I know the astronauts are inspiring him too, because three weeks earlier the successful Apollo mission captivated us all. To go beyond what is humanly possible calls for belief and hard work, on top of Mum's common sense.

Unusually, Mum stands up to Dad and moves into the attack: *'Don't make me spell it out. The children could drown, and this is totally irresponsible!'*

With a glint in his dark brown eyes, Dad turns to us: *'What do you want to do kids?'* He is making his four children, aged 15, 14, 12 and 10, into a little Executive Committee, with special responsibility to decide whether to swim across strong tidal currents.

I want to swim, and the adults are standing back, so we have to choose between them: the safe but unattractive choice is kinder to Mum, but disloyal to Dad.

My fifteen-year-old sister and twelve-year-old brother say yes to swimming, and I say yes too. We check with Dad: *'Can we all swim together please?'*

This is for safety, and also in deference to Mum.

Dad gives a cursory nod, then Mum grabs my ten-year-old brother and heads briskly back to the car.

So it is settled. We change into our swimming gear and tiptoe over the gravel, sand and seaweed into the water.

We begin swimming together as agreed, a line of four doing a steady breaststroke. Dad and my sister, who are the stronger swimmers, creep ahead leaving me and my brother trailing. A quick glance over the shoulder shows the north shoreline receding, but, disconcertingly, the far shore is getting no closer. I flip onto my back to rest my arms. The clouds have cleared making me tiny under a vast blue sky. I flip onto my front again, then, alarmingly, the other three swimmers have disappeared.

The line of boats in front is rushing towards the open sea, their mooring ropes rigid before them like sticks. Am I hallucinating? No, because a few moments later I figure it out: the river is widening, the boats are anchored, and I am hurtling upriver past them into treacherous currents where the in-pouring tide fights with the outflowing river.

There is a distant yell. *'Grab a boat!'* It is my brother.

Taking his advice, my last ounce of energy is spent front-crawling towards a boat that appears to be rushing menacingly towards me, its green slimy mooring rope rigid in front. I grab the rope, and, planting my feet on the shiny white hull, I haul myself out of rushing water onto the deck. With heart pounding, I lie on my back to recover, then stand straining in the bright, reflected sunlight to search for my brother. I'm guessing he is safe on a boat, but there are lots of boats. After a few minutes, I spot him on a distant deck, standing with hands shielding his eyes from the glare, gazing back at me. I point down and shout: *'Stay where you are!'* His thumbs-up tells me *'OK'*. There is no sign of Dad and my sister who left us behind.

At first I shiver, with salty, goose-pimpled skin, but soon I warm up and start to burn in the sun. It seems like hours before a battered launch comes puttering out of nowhere. I wave my arms and, as the boat approaches, the weather-beaten old fisherman steering it begins to rant angrily. I can't make out his words.

I climb aboard, and point to my brother. We rescue him, and then head out against a strong current towards the sea, searching all the anchored boats. Eventually we find my sister and my Dad, stranded separately. Ten minutes or so later, the fisherman unloads four crestfallen swimmers to the safety of the southern shore.

When we arrive, Mum and my younger brother are sitting in the front of the car. They have driven via Woodbridge to our landing point. Dad climbs into the backseat behind Mum, surrendering his usual position as driver, without protest. I sit in the middle with my big sister on the left. My middle brother spreads out in the luggage space behind.

By that time, it is far too late to go to the beach, and we drive back to the campsite in silence. Dad is just staring ahead, with a faint grin that betrays his private victory.

The Deben Estuary changed us that day, but I assumed that

sooner or later we would recover and regroup.

# Chapter 2: Silence

As we drive back via Woodbridge to the Hollesley camp, I am still mentally stranded on a boat deck, distanced from my family, with no one to rely on. I feel cold and alone. I badly need to assimilate what has just occurred.

My head is spinning with questions. It isn't too late to work out what mistakes we made, and to forgive each other, but who has the appetite? This is the start of an uncomfortable silence.

I always assumed I was born of a golden love affair into a blessed family, but the calamity at Deben Estuary brought an end to that hallowed sense of childhood.

Our family was nothing out of the ordinary. Until the generation before me, we'd scarcely entered the professions, and we'd occupied a scattering of jobs: a furniture mover, a shopkeeper, a baker/confectioner, a bookbinder/finisher, a post office overseer, a policeman, a travelling salesman and a café owner. More recently we'd had an accountant, a civil servant, an army officer, a shipping executive, plus some lawyers and teachers. Mum had been saved from biting poverty by a scholarship to a boarding school, and she sent us to the local state schools and we all passed into the grammar stream.

We shared an unusually strong interest in music. Mum played the piano, and her father used to sing in light opera on the stage in Reading. Grandma was an outstanding pianist, Dad loved to sing Gilbert and Sullivan, and between the four children we covered the recorder, violin, guitar, piano, cello and drums.

Because of Dad, we also stood out for our quirky interest in cars. Those old cars were always breaking down, and we got through a lot of them. It became a competition to memorise all the colours, makes, models, number plates, engine sizes and top speeds. We learned the best features of all the cars we ever owned, and many more besides.

Dad was a statistician and Mum said he had ants in his pants because he was easily bored. His career began in 1944 with four years' national service in the RAF, and thereafter he moved jobs at four-yearly intervals, continuing with the General Electric Company at Wembley where he analysed the results of trials in their research labs. That's where he met Mum. In 1952, he moved to Southern Electricity Board in Maidenhead, working on the tariffs and customer survey statistics. In 1956, at the National Coal Board his field was pneumoconiosis and the statistics related to miners' health. In 1960, at the Reed Paper Group he worked in paper factories to develop new packaging methods, like fibreboard and corrugated cardboard. Then he broke the mould by staying at Reed for eight years, and by moving from the field of statistics into something quite different called "management training". When he eventually left Reeds in 1968, he switched to a completely new line as a senior lecturer in management studies, in the social sciences faculty of a London polytechnic.

Our slightly geeky interests in music and cars were not what set us apart from the others we mingled with at school. Our family considered themselves to be good, honest churchgoers. Our behaviour was to be beyond reproach, and we were not to copy the mistaken behaviour of others. I accepted this uncomfortable position between naivety, obedience and self-righteous obsession. It was a complicated place to dwell, but this was who we were, until the Deben Estuary incident.

When Mum and Dad gave us no words of explanation for their difference of opinion on that riverbank, I lost the plot. They wanted to pretend it didn't matter, but it did. Their silence on the matter was worse than a terrible family row. Any story is better than no story: armed with a story you can claim your place, and figure out who you are.

Silence doesn't become more comfortable with the passing of time: the questions continue nagging. This was my experience throughout the thirty-one years until Dad died, and long afterwards. It was inevitable that eventually I would go looking for the truth.

Dad was pulling away, and he was less perfect than he pretended. He expected the children to tell the truth, while he was free to lie. He exempted himself from his own high moral standards, and he didn't wish anyone to point to this hypocrisy.

Dad's mathematician's mind could reduce complex questions about human nature to theories and beliefs that utterly missed the point, often diminishing Mum, and making us shrink from his impossible demands.

You might get a whiff of psychology here. It was never my plan to follow Dad into this awkward subject, but I was drawn into it by the Deben Estuary incident and other unexplained childhood events. I needed to feel secure. When I met Helen at university, she could look at strangers on the street and confidently describe who they were, where they were going and why. She was often right, because she knew about families, while I didn't have a clue. With her beside me something clicked, and I felt less alone.

When Helen and I went on honeymoon to California, I expected the full story of my childhood would come tumbling out from the part of my family residing there. But they didn't have a clue either.

Later, when we became parents ourselves to two children, my questions hadn't entirely gone away. I reflected on why. There's a little lost child inside each of us, who needs a narrative to bind them into a larger "us". Then they feel well-connected, secure and ready to go out into the world at their best. A parent shouldn't leave their child in the dark, because it holds them back in unseen ways.

Although a parent should shine a light and point the way, in the end it's the child who has to find their own answers, and so far I'd failed to do so.

I'd left it very late to get to the bottom of my questions and the obstacles only increased with the passing of time. Painstaking effort yielded a shred of information here and there, but the deeper understanding I sought proved impossible to achieve. Perhaps that's why this went on the back burner: life was busy enough.

As I approached forty in 1995, I started to keep a journal to ponder about why Dad's wheels fell off at that milestone age. If it was something genetic or chemical, I couldn't do much about that, but more likely Dad was sabotaging himself. The prop of writing reflectively kept me in good shape: happy at home and creative at work.

I didn't arrive at the deeper understanding, until rather later.

# Chapter 3: Respecting

Five years later, in November 2000, Dad died, and as his eldest I was asked to deliver a eulogy.

A eulogy is for honouring a life, but how can we praise someone towards whom we have mixed feelings? To choose just the good bits is disingenuous, and I needed to respect others present who were tangled up in Dad's life, whose best bits were my worst bits.

My children hardly got to know this Granddad-With-The-Black-Hair because Helen and I believed the other two Granddads were enough, the one with the pipe and the one with the beard. This third Granddad was a bundle of complications and a man they never knew.

My first draft was forthright:

> *I know little of the hand you were dealt. You have some good points: you were generous, brave and a pioneer, but like a moth to a flame. You wanted to live creatively, from the heart, very radical. Society was heaving and shifting in the Sixties, and you believed a better world was possible.*

> *But some parts are best glossed over, and some entirely forgiven.*

> *We lived together under the same roof and I knew where you stood, until you lost yourself then we lost each other. I needed to hear these words from you: 'I am your father, I will always be here for you'. I'm sad because this wasn't possible for you to say, and anyway it wasn't true.*

> *You found it more important to push the boundaries, throwing out what you called dusty old conventions. You destroyed our trust and failed to notice. But with your example I have moved into a different space less idealistic with a larger dose of practicality. Like you, I also want to give life to dreams, but not to chase dreams so radical they squash out the life.*

The eulogy I actually delivered at St Peters Church, Seaford on

Thursday 30th November 2000, was toned down and I hope more sympathetic:

*Your life was not a soft, dull and tasteless Golden Delicious but more 'in your face', a crisp, bitter-sweet Cox's Orange Pippin.*

*This eulogy is to praise you and your life with us. We could just mention the sweet bits and overdo the praise. But this would not respect your essence. So I will include the true tangy flavours.*

*You were the weather system bringing the sunshine and the storms.*

*You were the sunshine at the centre of my life and I was near the centre of yours. I wanted to be with you, digging the garden, cycling, swimming, mixing concrete, or fishing in the sea for prawns.*

*You also brought storms: when I refused the cabbage at Sunday lunch and you sent me away without pudding.*

*When you moved your sunshine and storms to others, I was sidelined. You left this bitter-sweet taste: happy memories plus unfinished business.*

*Of course there is good and bad in everything and everyone. You taught me to sing and to wire a plug. You gave me a scary experience in swimming an estuary and this built resilience.*

*You gave me vivid examples and choices. You pushed fearlessly beyond: instead of 'be careful', you said 'why not try'. You crashed a plane, you worked in Africa and climbed Kilimanjaro. You never stopped searching for life, the universe and everything.*

*Last weekend at our fireside, I was hunched over writing this, when my child said 'You're sucked into your work again'. I put down the laptop and brought the child to the centre of my attention. You inspired this by doing the*

*opposite and that lesson was much more powerful than
any of the theories you brought home.*

*You tried to rebuild bridges without admitting it was you
who destroyed them. It was hard for us to hug you back.
That is a sadness we can set aside for a sweeter taste in
this new phase.*

*So what would you want from us here at your memorial
service? Not much really. To sing our hearts out. Not
to make a fuss. To remember you with respect and
understanding. To be kind to one another.*

As I was leaving the church afterwards, the priest asked if I was
angry. I said do you think I am? He said yes. I asked how he
knew. He said I gave the eulogy without breaking down. I said
I cried earlier, which was true. I asked do people always break
down. He said yes as soon as they are ready to let go.

After the service, my brothers were encouraging and grateful
the eulogy did not fall to them, and I appreciated their support.
I had broken, if only briefly, the silence that started after
the estuary, but I'd had enough of thinking about Dad. The
necessary ordeals had been completed and I hoped to continue
life in peace.

But the priest's opinion gave me an uneasy feeling that I was still
entangled with Dad, and it might not be easy to break free.

## Chapter 4: The Itch

During tea after the funeral, the invitation came from Dad's third wife to pick up a few things Dad had left for us. Two weeks later, we called at her house, where she handed over a few management books and a black metal box. It was nothing of any value, she said, just old family things.

When we got the box home, I found old diaries and family photos inside. I sorted the photos into a pile for each brother, then closed the box, with a string of excuses to myself: I didn't want to read the diaries. I was too busy. It didn't matter any more. I didn't want to disturb fond family memories. Our lives were too full with the pressing demands of young children.

That is why I put the black metal box out of sight in the attic. I guessed there might be something in it Dad wanted me to see, but I was wary and defiant: Dad had left it too late.

The box remained there in the attic, untouched for fifteen years. Out of sight isn't always out of mind though, and a nagging question kept coming back: why did my parents really split up?

In Easter 2009, more than eight years after Dad's memorial service, we visited my cousins in Perth, Australia. During this visit, Dad's sister Auntie M kindly offered to answer any family questions *'while she still could'*. It was an opportunity not to miss.

Auntie M with her husband Uncle D treated us to a Swan River Wine Cruise, with buffet, and winery tour thrown in. The river setting outside was beautiful, and inside the boat we sat comfortably before a starched white tablecloth, laden with salmon, salads, and Sauvignon Blanc. The most delightful part was the prospect of answers to my pressing family questions.

When Auntie said she was ready I started with the first question: *'Why did my parents split up?'*
The answer flew off her tongue: *'The split was triggered when your sister died'*.

My sister died back in September 1971 and I was seventeen.

There we were, thirty-eight years later in 2009, sitting on the river cruise, and it was the first time anyone had offered to explain. What's more, Auntie M's explanation made sense. When a child dies, it is hard for the parents to bear. They grieve differently and, unable to support one another, they fall apart. So, my sister's death was the reason my parents broke up, and it was a relief to have this answer.

To be sure, I wanted to eliminate some other possible reasons, but Auntie M refused: *'I won't be cross-examined'*.

We moved on to my second pressing question: *'What caused my sister's death?'* Over the years since 1971, the answer had become confused in my mind: there was a "First Diagnosis", then a "Second Opinion" and an abrupt move to a different hospital. Then I remembered silence on this topic too.

Again Auntie M had the answer ready: *'Ovarian Cancer was the cause of death'*.

Inwardly I protested, because Ovarian Cancer was just the first diagnosis, and everyone said this was very rare for a girl of that age. I was certain Auntie M was wrong with this one, because the "Second Opinion" was different. Privately, I labelled Auntie M's explanation a "harmless lie".

The cruise continued, and Auntie refused to be drawn further on those two questions. I found out that Auntie M knew nothing of the Deben Estuary swim, and little about certain other family matters, but she filled me in on Dad's qualities as a child. Auntie M spoke of harsh punishments from their father for not eating their vegetables. I noticed how this particular punishment had passed down the generations. When Uncle D got to know Dad as an adult, he noticed *'blanks on his screen'*. Dad's *'naivety'* made it impossible to continue their friendship.

We saw little of the Swan River that day, but I gained a much better understanding of Dad's upbringing and the early years of his marriage to Mum.

As soon as we got back to our hotel, I sat down eagerly to make notes. I trusted Auntie M, a trained lawyer who worked with solid evidence, but the crispness of her answers left a small seed of doubt, and caused me to reflect: how could the itchy questions that had plagued me for so many years be so easily settled?

To blame the marriage break up on my sister's death was a relief in some ways. This neatly explained the marriage crisis and removed any blame from Mum and Dad. It cleared up a lot of confusion. But inwardly I refused to accept it. How could they blame a child? This lie wasn't harmless like the first one because it wronged my sister who could no longer defend herself. I put this explanation down as "convenient".

I was already certain that my sister's death was not the first crisis in my parents' marriage. I needed to tidy the muddle in my mind, and get to the truth. I imagined confronting Dad in a court, although he was long dead by then, because I wanted to overturn those two lies: the harmless lie and the convenient lie.

Before we left for the airport, Auntie M handed us Grandpa's war medals including an Imperial Service Order awarded in October 1954 while he was in the rank of Lieutenant Colonel, and two earlier mentions in Despatches in December 1941 and January 1944.

I was to keep the medals safely to pass on for future generations, but this raised another problem: how to answer the questions my children would obviously raise. They would ask: *'What did Grandpa do to get these medals?' 'Why is it so important to keep them safely?'* Auntie M included newspaper clippings with explanations vague enough to make my children's eyes glaze over. I imagined answering my children's questions flippantly, saying unlike the rest of us Grandpa was too big to go down the plughole.

During the long flight home, I was weighed down by a "harmless lie" about my sister's death, a "convenient lie" about my parents' break up, Grandpa's medals and an itch that hadn't gone away. I wanted to overturn those lies. I wanted to give my children all the necessary information about Grandpa and the medals because, I told myself, the passer-on of medals has a larger role as the passer-on of stories. I noticed I was starting to like Dad rather less, and Mum rather more.

THE IMPERIAL SERVICE ORDER.

The Badge should be worn in the following manner:—

And a new nagging question arose: what is a father for?

*

One evening Helen and I were chatting with two old friends over a beer in our local pub garden. They raised the subject: *'What do you think about fathers?'*

A single word came to my lips: *'Admiration'*
Then Helen threw something in: *'But your Dad died a lonely man'.*

Perceptively our friend said: *'So your Dad's not simply a good guy'.*
I moved into defence: *'OK, he wasn't simply a good guy, but he*

*wasn't such a bad guy either'*. Unlike many, Dad did actually feature in my life. It was how he featured that was problematic.

During the ensuing discussion, the dads were shown to be more disastrous than the mums. Dads walk away, and can be walked away from, but that's not necessarily bad. Dad is the giver of sperm, but beyond that his behaviour can be random: fun or violent, simply unreliable or more seriously cruel. Deceit and disappointment feature, as do painful departures, inexplicable absences, and unwelcome returns.

Dads are fated to be like that, although many of us hope to be better.

Our friend confessed: *'I also have a foolish admiration for my Dad'*. He told us his dad was comically unpredictable, going to bed at any time of day while fully dressed in a smart work suit.

On the way home, Helen said: *'This admiration for your Dad is wearing a bit thin'*.
I held her hand, and felt foolish: *'Do you think they noticed?'*
The conversation in the pub had exposed my *'admiration'* as covering up something more sour, and what still rankled was Dad's inexplicable silence.

Helen said: *'Like father like son'*. She didn't say more, and nor did I.
I didn't defend myself because my head was spinning with a confusion that I'll go on to describe.

I'm sure you can picture us. Two empty-nesters walking home from the pub in South West London. What are we seeing? Victorian streets lined with rarely used cars, parked amongst builders' vans and skips. Low gardens walls just a stride from the front door, past all the recycling bins. We step along dark halls, towards lively family gatherings in lighter more modern rear extensions with kitchen cum dining cum seating spaces, spilling onto patios with parasols and patches of lawn. When the children leave, it doesn't feel so crowded.

Our children were the whirlwinds that swept into this place, carrying us through the infancy, schools, and the homes of their friends, before they left for university with their sights on jobs, homes and partners of their own.

From the miracle moment when a tiny new life begins, no parental plan ever stands up to what life throws at it. With no job description there is no one right way. We do our best while most of us don't have a clue.

As we repeat the family cycle, we are sucked into the pressing business of daily life, with only the tiniest room to adjust. A thousand invisible threads connect the past, present and future. But can we grab hold of those hidden threads? Or do we trust our parenting to fate?

We all just disappear in the end, but before we do we will look back upstream and ask what did our parents pass to us. It's only natural to ask what shall I pass on, and I say it's your job as an adult to pass on the threads of your story, before you go and time washes everyone and everything down the plughole.

But Dad never gave me the threads of his story, and perhaps that's why he never washes away. I can't erase what I know of him because his life is inseparable from mine until I have worked out which parts I want to keep, and I'll ditch quite a lot because I refuse to end up like him.

I'm sad that my children without their granddad's story are blind to a part of themselves, and to a quarter of their DNA.

After the pub garden, the bottom line was becoming clear: I would go to extreme lengths to find the threads to cling onto. Those threads are part of an adult's equipment for life. Dad's life would be a caution. I would write down his story and check myself, to be sure I am different. I would let my children read it too.

But this was 2009, and back then I didn't have the time to follow through.

## Chapter 5: Peak Bubble

When we got to Majorca in May 2015, it was a pivotal moment. We were crossing a line.

The white stucco villa near the beach, with its garden and swimming pool was filled with happy people. Our children turned up, as energetic young adults with their other halves. We'd invited old friends too. What better way to celebrate my Sixtieth?

It was festive with coloured bunting. I was the guest. They cooked tapas with tortilla and albondigas, seafood paella, and a nice Rioja. We loaded up our favourite songs on YouTube. One song prompted another, and we were happily sozzled when we finally went to bed.

Phew, I thought, we had finally arrived after a lifetime of work to a relaxed way of living. We enjoyed a rare moment of fruition, filled with a sense of achievement.

But we were not ready for endless days of sunshine and sparkling wine. I called this time "Peak Bubble" because something was about to burst.

*

A few days later we were home again. We were no longer ourselves. I dug the flowerbeds and reflected. The kids were planted out long ago. We were making moves to retire. Time was hanging heavy. Why was everything good unravelling? Our social life was changing, with "first world problems" souring each friendly chat.

Helen's hip was part of it too, flaring up so inexplicably after a walk along the Thames. I watched her hobbling in pain with that stick. She was asking: *'What's next?'* This spurred us on to do what's important while we still could. We kept asking ourselves: *'What's really important right now?'*

When my spade struck something hard, I smiled with recognition. I dug out the object with a trowel and brushed off the earth. Its red and white Gingham lid was clogged with rust, and I forced it off.

Twenty years ago, our children put their special treasures into this jar, once sparkling and full of French peach jam. Why? To give alien visitors the necessary clues about human life on earth. It was a time capsule.

I squatted on the lawn and pulled out a conker, a picture of Thomas the Tank Engine and a toy soldier with white plastic parachute, but I had to leave the sticky sweet melted inside. The day we put this together, the children took turns to stand on the kitchen chair and release the soldier with its carefully packed parachute. We watched it spiral and crash to the floor. With childlike naivety we repeated this tirelessly, and the soldier never landed well.

When I fished out those objects, earlier memories poured into me, of my parents who perfectly supported my young life. Dad's joyful spontaneity was perfectly balanced against Mum's thoughtful caution.

These childhood memories too often invaded our most

enjoyable moments, as if they belonged with us still.

Out of nowhere, a new, possibly mad idea arrived. Why not welcome these old memories, instead of trying in vain to push them away? Why not give them a place at our table? Why not honour them like guests? Perhaps we could settle them with gentle questions and a more generous space for expression.

This is exactly what I resolved to do, and it also provided a way to piece together the stories that I wanted to pass on.

There I was, squatting on the lawn with knees aching, repacking my children's treasures into the jam jar, and imagining a time capsule of my own, containing the stories that needed to be told. A warm glow of optimism arrived because instead of pointlessly digging the garden, I was about to embark on something useful to our children, and for the greater good.

That is how a deflated day turned into a lovely evening. We went out onto the patio to drink Malbec. Helen was encouraging when I brought my proposal: *'It's better than playing victim!'*

We started fooling around, singing along to Sgt Pepper: *'We've got to admit it's getting better, getting so much better all the time!'*

As we imagined this adventure unfolding, a weight was being lifted. We decided to be time travellers, going back to the Sixties when, heady with optimism, people were building a better world to escape the threat of nuclear war.

Why would we do this? Because we could, it was going to be fun, and the adventure would be good for us. Also because an exorcism was required, and although we were not qualified to perform strange religious rites, we would fall back on what we knew. Like detectives, we would trace Dad's footsteps at the pivotal moments of my childhood. We would visit places and interview family members. I would write a journal of what we found. Helen and I would talk, we would dream and I would meditate. Using these methods we would stir the deeply buried memories and allow our creative minds to solve this. We would literally be "re-membering" Dad and I would be making peace with the past.

That evening was therapeutic: we started to smile, and at bedtime Helen threw her stick down and dared to walk unaided up the stairs. The following day, Helen the great hater of long haul, said: *'Let's begin, while my hip still allows it'.*

This was May 2015. Our happy bubble had burst and the former life was well and truly over. Freed from work, we were getting ready to travel to distant continents to be detectives, psychologists, dramatists and narrators to scrape away the accretion of sediment and dig up remnants, ready to piece together treasures from the past.

From that moment, we were on a "quest", and we shared a sense of urgency: we would not be timed out, and what had recently been a persistent itch was at last given some proper attention.

Part Two:

# Setting The Stage

## Chapter 6: Weddings, War Heroes and Wonder Women

It was June 2015. We wanted to welcome back old memories like guests into our home, and we had some practical ideas about how to move forward.

We went to our coffee table full of photographs. These featured our own young family, right up until the day when digital cameras took over. Here we also kept the older photo albums, left to us by deceased relatives, going back a century.

Helen and I were browsing through the old photos, and unlocking memories. *'It's just a family puzzle'*, she said. We chose to begin with the big events. The family tree I drew up the previous summer helped us get to know the characters. Through common sense, an intelligent approach and a critical eye, we were confident we could uncover what was driving those events.

The first big event was the wedding in September 1949, four years after the war. We placed the black and white photograph on the tabletop and took turns with a magnifying glass.

Twenty-six smiling people are standing outside a Methodist church in Wembley, ten of them men, in dark suits and ties, their hair short and combed back. The fifteen women wear hats, gloves, little handbags, and flat black shoes. The dresses are varied and below the knee. There is just one child.

My parents in the centre are young, slim and happy. Mum has white ribbons in her thick wavy hair, a simple pearl necklace and an off-white dress, ruched with zigzag stitching at the waist. Ten white roses on her left arm, her right hand in a white lace glove is through Dad's left arm, and her head inclines slightly towards him. Dad wears a double-breasted, pinstripe with wide lapels, a white carnation, and a gentle smile.

We started speculating about the two families. The fathers of both bride and groom served in the First World War, Mum's was in the Navy and Dad's was in the Army. Mum's was the less lucky father, shipwrecked and wounded, and after the war his mounting difficulties drove him to run away, thus casting the family into the jaws of poverty. By contrast, Dad's father returned intact into a demanding and successful career in the War Office and his family prospered. I was lucky because of that. Both bride and groom had experienced many years of their childhood without a father: the groom because of a career and the bride because of an unexplained disappearance. We were setting the scene for a tragedy.

But how could we understand Mum and Dad's world in 1949? We turned to the Internet. I imagined introducing this portal to Dad: a vast encyclopaedia with every known fact, a book of all human history, an R&D lab for every specialist inquiry, a university with access to every professor's work, a hospital with treatments for every ailment, a two-way channel to communicate with almost anyone in the world, and a funding source for any unaffordable project. We had the reach and access previously confined to sovereigns, presidents, popes and CEOs. Dad would have found this terrifically exciting.

Online, we dug out the key facts about 1949. Money was short and expectations high. The National Health Service was just born, and the railways nationalised. People were paranoid about the spread of communism, and Britain was forming NATO with the Americans to drive away the Russians. There were lots of firsts: a first laundrette, a first computer, the maiden flight of a passenger jet, the first Secret Seven story by Enid Blyton, and the first TV broadcast beyond London.

We returned to the photo.

*

Dad is standing between his mother and the bride. Appropriately somehow, Dad's father is looking on from the rear. Mum has a bridesmaid to her left, then it's her mother, and next surprisingly is Auntie M, Dad's immaculately dressed sister, placing herself on the bride's side of the group, not far from Mum's tall younger brother.

Mum's off-white dress implies a previous relationship.

*

We dragged ourselves back to 2015, and researched pre-marital relationships. A scandalous sex survey in 1949 had challenged the "virgin bride" ideal. Over half the women in Britain had pre-marital sex, and men's sexual experiences in the war included prostitutes and homosexuality. Those survey results were so shocking they had to be locked away in a university vault for fifty years.

The women outnumbered the men in the wedding photo, perhaps on account of the war, and we registered some notable absences. Dad's brother, Uncle R, was absent doing National Service. Mum's father was missing because he ran away over twenty years earlier, still shell-shocked after the First World War, so Mum's brother stood in and gave the bride away. How did the other guests regard those two absentees? We speculated. The National Service would be considered dutiful but the running away shameful, and from this, glory landed on Dad's family but shame landed on Mum's. It didn't show on their faces, and those in this crowd are now dubbed the "silent generation".

Four glittering women stood out in my young life. The first in order of birth, Auntie G, was Mum's elder sister, but she was missing from the photo for a good reason: she had recently sailed to Nairobi, to be with her husband, an ex-RAF pilot. With a fashionable hat, bobbed hair, floaty dresses, and an exotic cigarette in a pastel shade, everything would have matched. Born in 1920, Auntie G was a Soroptimist campaigning to improve the lives of girls and women worldwide. Her RAF pilot husband shot down in the war was held in a prison of war camp. He returned a bit of a hero.

Mum herself was the second glittering "wonder woman", not for her dresses but for her successful entry into medicine when the profession was almost exclusively male. After leaving school in 1941, she tried nursing, then lodged in Harrow and worked in research while she studied part-time to become a GP. Driving the Red Cross ambulance during the night air raids in London made her a bit of a heroine too.

Mum didn't talk about her missing years between 1941 and 1948, but Auntie G hinted there was a relationship, and Auntie M said Mum's close friend, Joan, tried to block the marriage, but the details didn't matter.

The third glittering woman was Auntie C, Mum's glamorous younger sister. Helen and I had raised our eyebrows during our honeymoon in 1980, when Auntie C showed us shots of herself naked, taken by a photographer in Reading. This was just before she was married, at the age of eighteen, to an American GI. This older man, recently divorced and father to a young child, was my Uncle J, a scientist who had us believe he contributed a great deal to the war.

Auntie C wasn't at the wedding either, because in 1945 she had taken the liner to her new life with Uncle J in the USA.

Those first three "wonder women" grew up without a father, without a stable home or a steady income. Their tall younger brother who gave Mum away at the wedding, was a marine commando whose covert missions in northern France supported the Normandy landings and turned the tide of the war.

The fourth glittering woman was Auntie M, Dad's sister, who became a close friend to Mum. Auntie M was on the front row of the photo, standing surprisingly on the side of the bride's family. The father she shared with Dad, in the back row of the photo, was a hero in both world wars. Shortly after the wedding, Auntie M flitted to Africa for a teaching job and disobeyed her father's instruction to return. She married an Irishman in Uganda (Uncle D), they had three sons and, after they moved the family to Australia, Auntie M qualified as a barrister.

Despite the distances, these four women stayed in touch with Mum, in a special way. What bound them together? I can say that whenever Mum was with a "wonder woman", the conversation became different. There was a special excitement in the voices, sliding in and out of hushed whispers. The eyes would be glittery or watery. They were the first generation of women born with the vote, the first wives whose vows did not require them to obey their husbands, driving a path through the "patriarchy" and punching above their weight. They spoke in code to hide from an eavesdropping child or a husband, exchanging secrets on such topics as when to surrender, when to fight back, and how much suffering to bear, as the unpredictable storms of change blew into their marriages.

Those four women knew Dad well enough, and better than that, they also knew Mum's point of view. Their insights could be invaluable towards our quest, that is why Helen and I tried to find them, but it wasn't so simple in the end.

*

We were on the point of visiting Auntie G, in early July 2015, to put our questions about Dad, but her death denied us the chance. We attended her funeral in Yorkshire, and returned a fortnight later to visit S (Auntie G's daughter in law), the one closest to Auntie G at the end.

Surprisingly for Yorkshire, the sun was shining. We were taking a vineyard tour with S on the windswept Pennine Hills wondering how the grapes could possibly grow. Panoramic sunlit views and some great lines from the tour guide were making us hopeful our trip wasn't going to be in vain. As we sat down in the café,

S opened her bag and handed over family photos she had put aside for us from Auntie G's collection. Disappointingly she steered clear of my questions, and the silence was with me again. Perhaps S had good reasons for this evasion. She hadn't exactly cast Dad into shame, but there was a nasty smell surrounding him that S preferred not to name.

After a pleasant afternoon we went our separate ways and headed home. Later that evening we looked through the photos S passed us. There was little trace of Dad except for a chilling family photo in which his face was scribbled out with blue biro. I found a roughly typed note from Auntie G written just before Mum's funeral in 2002 headed "Recollections Of A Sister". She said Mum *'fell head over heels'* for Dad. He made her laugh and their physical attraction was obvious. But when the four children arrived, Mum was *'over-tolerant'*, while Dad indulged himself in every possible extra-curricular activity including cricket, tennis, music, politics and the church. Mum had no time to rest after all her doctoring work followed by all the housework, and she was exhausted.

Helen summarised it neatly: *'So Fun Dad morphed into Neglectful and Irresponsible Dad'.*

*

Helen and I had met the second "wonder woman" during our honeymoon in California in 1980. Auntie C died shortly afterwards in 1984, but we met her daughter, Cousin M, several times, both in Egypt where she lived, and on her visits to the UK.

Cousin M was born in San Diego, California, six months before my parents' wedding, then emigrated to Canada, and married an Egyptian. They moved to Egypt and raised two kids. When her husband died she took up a rural smallholding.

Once, when we flew out to see her in Cairo, Cousin M picked us up from our airport hotel in her dusty bronze Jeep Cherokee and drove us out of the city southwards along the banks of the Nile towards her farm.

While driving, Cousin M delivered a history of the involvement of the British in this region. It was complex and violent. As a convert to Islam, she gave us new perspectives. Outside the Jeep, farmers were driving donkeys laden with vegetables from the green fields, their ancient way of life plainly outlasting the centuries of man-made catastrophes.

Suddenly, the jeep was off the road and hurtling through a missing section of chainlink fence, and Cousin M was racing confidently up and down the Sahara sand dunes, towards pyramids more ancient than the famous ones at Giza: a stepped one, a bent one and a red one. We stopped and walked up close to survey each structure's uniqueness and immensity. We saw diggings as recent as last night and as ancient as the nineteenth century. These blatant plunderings of the national heritage were said to bring on the curse of the pharaohs.

When we returned through the chainlink fence onto the road, Cousin M's farm was just a short drive along the green fertile strip squeezed between river and desert. She had built two single storey houses  and lived there with three parrots, sixteen rat terriers, twenty horses, two water buffalo, an Afghan hound, plus a small staff.

The informative monologue continued as we entered her home. I handed over single malt whisky from the airport, and seized the moment to leap in with our questions:

*'What do you remember of my Dad?'*

Cousin M remembered one small thing. When her family came to visit us in 1965, Dad showed them round the paper factory where he worked. He pointed to a hot bubbling tub of paper pulp and said: *'Careful. You'll not last long if you throw yourself in there'.*

He might have been talking about the mayhem he threw himself into shortly afterwards.

*A few years later in 1971, I visited with my brothers Cousin M's family in California, and I wondered why Cousin M wasn't there:*

*'Can you say what made you leave California?'*

Cousin M replied darkly with remarks about a *'military-industrial complex'* that created the debacle of Vietnam. The wars in Iraq and Afghanistan were signs of that "complex" gearing itself up again. She felt better off in Egypt cut adrift from the mainstream, surrounding herself with animals, far from the madness. She refused to follow the norm.

I pulled back to the question: *'Was it the Vietnam draft that drove you away?'*
Cousin M re-focused: *'Right. My boyfriend was draft dodging. My father was in the military, on missile-tracking systems. He went to conferences about cybernetics and anthropology, hanging out with Margaret Mead and other high falutin' folks'.*

I remember Cousin M's father, Uncle J, sitting at a picnic table outside their family house in Ojai, California in 1971. By then Cousin M had departed for Canada. Uncle J told me he was *'just an old man'* who liked to hang out with young university students at Stanford and Berkeley, chatting on the *'trunk'* of his car: *'their young minds were captivating'*.

Cousin M added something about Margaret Mead, the anthropologist, whose ideas about a permissive society were sending her father slightly crazy. He left his job as a US government research scientist and set off towards Canada in a camper van. She said her father was *'complicated and quite nasty'*. He returned to California sometime in the mid-1970s with a brain tumour, and died.

During our honeymoon in 1980, Uncle J was long dead, and Helen and I were visiting Cousin M's mother (Auntie C) who claimed she was perfectly happy living in the trailer park. She showed us a shoebox of photographs rescued from a fire in the family house, and told us proudly of Uncle J's project to build human colonies under the sea, but all his papers had been lost in the fire.

Cousin M had nothing more about Dad, and perhaps her "dad issues" were weightier than mine. She drove us back towards our hotel in Cairo, and we stopped for dinner on the way, during which Cousin M told us more about her life in Egypt including her horses and the desert trails rides she offers.

*

We paid a visit to Dad's younger brother, Uncle R, who missed the wedding due to National Service. Since the death of his wife, he was living on his own near Southampton.

When we arrived, R had laid out a buffet tea and was ready with old family photographs and a memorable story.

It was September 1952 when R came to visit my parents in their rented flat in Maidenhead, three years into my parents' marriage. It was a Friday and that evening they all went to Dad's company dance, where Dad introduced R to a single girl who had recently arrived in his office. The next day, it was Saturday afternoon and Mum was studying at medical school in London, while Dad and R occupied themselves. Mum returned to find Dad with a big smile on his face, standing beside his embarrassed brother and, as R put it, *'hundreds of photographs of women'*. Every surface including the floor was covered.

Mum, whose days as a trainee female doctor consisted of routine humiliations by the cosy, male, sexist establishment, was unimpressed. She cast her eyes around the room and demanded an explanation. Dad said:

*'We are trying to choose the perfect wife for R, and we are approaching it scientifically, by rating each woman on a ten point scale'.*

Uncle R protested this was unnecessary, because he was very happy with the girl he met the previous night at the dance. But Dad insisted they show Mum exactly how the scoring worked.

Uncle R refused to score the women, and Dad ran through a few pictures calling out the scores he felt they deserved, until Mum stopped the game. Uncle R then discretely left for a walk, allowing Mum, who was furious, the chance to extract an explanation.

Uncle R never found out where Dad got the photos from, but perhaps it wasn't unusual for men to put together such a stash. Dad's game with "hot or not" ratings, was a pre-technology FaceMash, the predecessor of Facebook, which allowed Harvard students to post ratings for the attractiveness of their peers.

*

Back home after these visits, Helen and I reflected on our progress, or lack of it.

When Dad married Mum, the new brothers-in-law had played big parts in the war effort, as had Mum with her ambulance driving in the blitz. Being younger, Dad caught just the tail end of the war. He once crash-landed a plane, which is kind of heroic too isn't it?

He was not an easy husband though, and Mum sometimes appreciated the support she received from the "wonder women".

# Chapter 7: Humpback Bridges

In July 2015, we found another way to keep the quest moving.

*'What's your earliest memory?'*

Helen's provocative question brought a surprising answer. It was oddly visceral, recorded deeply in my flesh and bones, and taking us back to 1959.

*

I am four years old, and squashed in the back seat of our black saloon, speeding towards the Sussex coast. My sister is in front, beside Dad who is driving, and I want to be there in the front, but I am in the back on the left. Mum is on the right, holding my baby brother. My other brother is in the middle, watching the road through a gap between the two front seats.

Dad sees a bridge ahead and speeds up. The car hits the hump and goes flying through the air, for a microsecond, but it feels like an eternity! Our hearts are in our mouths, filling the air with laughter and squealing. I see delight in our flashing eyes. We-are-one and the feeling is pure joy.

The car stops and we pose on the ladder of an old railway signal.

*

I paused to find an old colour photograph that popped into my mind. It was in a green album tied with a black plaited chord. We propped it up on the dining table to keep it on display. Mum's writing in white crayon on the black mounting paper said: '*Bluebell Railway, August 1959*'.

It was fifty-six years ago.

We looked carefully. The red and white arm of the signal was horizontal on a tall, white vertical post. I was at the top of the ladder, with my sister below. Our two young brothers were carried by my parents.

Helen was sceptical about my story, asking: *'What's really going on?'* She refused to believe the sweet harmony I described, because life was never like that, she said. She dug deeper for the gritty reality using awkward questions:

*'What happened after the car landed? What's going on behind those smiling faces?'*

Faced by Helen's doubt, random details about Dad began to flood back. He was the bringer of excitement, whirling small children in dizzying windmills and roundabouts. He was the instigator of jokes, pillow fights and party games. He was good. One memory triggers another.

I wrote all these memories straight down in a notebook, before they disappeared again. Then I tried to look more critically.

I loved studying the picture up close, but it didn't offer the answers to Helen's awkward questions. It struck me as interesting to re-draw the picture myself, so I downloaded a "sketcher" app onto the iPad and invested an afternoon to trace and fill in the outlines of each person. This calming practice brought something more: I remembered they used to call me

*'Sunny Jim'*. I felt like a time traveller sketching that small boy, Sunny Jim, as he went about his life in 1959.

The next morning, I awoke with remarkable new detail: the cars, the dates when we owned them, and the registration numbers. I'd once written them in my car-spotting book and memorised them. A light blue Mini van (1961?). A muddy green Hillman Husky (JJG 563). A Vauxhall Victor Estate in two-tone dark and light blue (688 KO, 1967-68). A turquoise Ford Cortina Estate (GGK 845C,1968-69). A grey Morris Traveller (729 AVX) with external wood trim and chrome "trafficator arms" that popped out, instead of indicator lights, to signal left or right.

I remembered the old Humber Super Snipe and rifled through the photo album to find a black and white picture of it: KTW 303. Spontaneously, more of the Humpback Bridge scene came back to me.

*

Dad is in grey trousers and white shirt with sleeves rolled up, his black hair neatly parted and brushed back, with his broad white smile of babyish teeth.

Mum, petite with soft hazel eyes and the thick mop of ginger hair, is in the backseat, holding my baby brother. She hates that expensive heavy car.

The flight lands with a bump, bringing giggles and groans, and the clasping of stomachs.

My sister says: *'I feel sick'*.
I say: *'Let me sit in the front then'*.
Mum says to Dad: *'Why did you **have to** do that?'*

\*

Mum's *'have to'* is what did produced Dad's next move, which was revealing and provocative.

\*

Dad turns round to his left and gives Sunny Jim a wink that says *'You and I are allies'*. Those two laugh for a long moment in complicity, until Dad returns his sparkling brown eyes onto the road. It's obvious that Mum is not with them, and does not share their joy.

\*

Helen's awkward questions, my careful sketching and a good night's sleep had combined to produce new layers of detail that were setting us on the right track. We could tell that the hump-back flight of pure joy was nothing of the kind: it produced a heavy landing and an all-too-familiar crash from joy into misery.

How had we arrived at this? Helen and I had stepped into the car, taken on the characters and felt the meaning of these events. From this vivid episode we learned so much.

Dad was the optimist, who loved throwing us into things, and there was no intended harm, because he believed God was protecting us. He contributed the wilder family excitement, and we needed that. But Mum, the pragmatist took on the necessary job of looking out for risks.

Mum dreaded each looming tragedy ahead, but despite this remained strong, protective, and determined to look after the children. She maintained her sense of humour, except when the family was under threat, laughing at Dad's dreadful jokes and shaking her curly head in mock despair.

Helen and I were delighted with our discovery. Each step towards the truth soothed me, as if I was releasing something tightly clenched inside.

## Chapter 8: Surreal Adventure

We entered August 2015 buoyed up by our discovery about the Humpback Bridge.

*'We have lots of resources,'* said Helen, *'and next we need to tap into your brothers'.* A chat over a pint was the obvious answer, but they lived several miles apart, so I arranged to see them separately.

I was the firstborn brother, followed after eighteen months by the second, and twenty-two months later by the third. We grew up together, six eyes in a little unit of three, constantly watching Dad, whether he was digging the garden or walking or changing the gears in the car. If Dad knew it or not, he was teaching us who we wanted to be.

My mind flashed back happily to the way we were.

*

Mum asks Dad anxiously: *'Do you know where The Boys are?'* Or *'What shall we do with The Boys?'* The Boys is the collective noun for us.

The Boys are a worry and a burden. Our games include slapping, knuckling, Chinese burns, arm-wrestling, dares, chicken, and later on smoking cigarettes and underage drinking. As small boys we crash our bicycles, burn ants using a magnifying glass, light small fires in The New Forest and compete to swim the farthest out to sea.

Mum encourages us to be one tight family: *'Make sure you play nicely'. 'Offer the sweets to each other, so that everyone gets their fair share.'* When one of The Boys is out of his depth, the others usually help. We are all for one and one for all.

The family is a lopsided triangle with The Boys doing their boisterous things, forgetting the rules laid down by The Parents, and ignoring our Sister's pleas to behave. Our Sister is different, being older and closer to The Parents.

The Boys are my playmates, co-conspirators, my escape from

boredom, my source of adventure, and the identity I enjoy. I belong with them, and to them. We are so much more than three individuals. We can do more together than apart.

*

Perhaps that was just in my dreams. As the meetings with my brothers approached, I was anxiously hoping to add pieces to the picture of our young life with Dad.

I began the first meeting, with a tightness in my throat and stomach, and a whine in my voice: *'No one ever talks about Dad and I don't know why'*.

This brother, who knows motorbikes, computers and music tossed his complaint back: *'Dad was a bodger. The cars he repaired would always break down again'*.
I nudged the topic forward: *'Do you remember swimming the estuary?'*
If he remembered he didn't let on: *'Dad never did anything properly'*.

Then the subject was closed.

My other brother was living in Bruges to escape the grind of life and UK's general air of moral decay. So he said.

I began guardedly, my voice a monotone: *'Do you remember when we went with Dad in the white camper van?'*
He ducked it: *'You're always analysing everything'*.
I complained bitterly: *'But no one ever talks about anything'*.

His defence was intriguing: *'I saw things I shouldn't have seen. I did things…'*. He trailed off, refusing to say more. Then I remembered how the adventure began: it was the summer of 1972, a Fiat camper van (EKL 513K), bound for Germany. Mum got out at Dover, taking herself home on the train. It was slightly alarming, to be left with Dad, who refused to tell us where we were going. He just said: *'Wait and see'*.

Memories can be surreal and easy to doubt. The camaraderie I once enjoyed with my brothers had become fragile, and I chose not to push them and spoil those rare moments together, although they were my only witnesses, . The quest was mine not theirs, and they had given us as much as they could.

I was hurt by their dismissal, but defiant and determined to speak about what actually happened back then. I reasoned that with Helen's help we could uncover the truth and by doing so we gave everyone, including ourselves, a chance to make the future better than the past. A true story opens a door to change, I said to myself, bringing everyone the potential to be better than they are. How could anyone argue with that?

But hang on, my voice, self-righteous and harping on about potential, was sounding rather like Dad.

## Chapter 9: Kenya

On a warm evening in September 2015, I was relaxing in the light breeze on the terrace of a Nairobi hotel, sipping a cool beer. The three-day meeting that brought me to Africa was over, allowing me precious moments to reflect on where we are going with the quest.

There was an underlying problem: we didn't have enough witnesses. My brothers couldn't help, and most of the others were dead. We were over-reliant on my memory, plus an auntie's point of view, and a few old photos. If we were to challenge that "convenient lie" about my parent's break-up, we needed solid evidence.

This district of Nairobi was named Uhuru, meaning "freedom", in celebration of Nairobi's independence from colonial domination, and a phrase rang in my head: *'when you truly want to break free, it is fragments of yourself you must discard'*. It made me think about Dad.

I went back in my mind to when I visited Kenya before.

*

It is 1975. I am nineteen, visiting Dad where he is training African managers in a college in Lower Kabete near Nairobi.

Dad has recently crashed, like the parachutist in the time capsule, and is trying to start all over again. He is caught in painful daily arguments with his new partner Shirley and their young sons. The family is sinking into debt while their income in Kenyan Shillings is shrinking against sterling.

Dad pretends he is well, but he plainly isn't and his optimism irritates me. He refuses to talk about how he landed in these dire straits. He distracts himself from the bleak truth by filling his days with work, learning Swahili and digging his garden. The new crop of bananas and yams is promising, but his new interests, in the I Ching and Transcendental Meditation, are flaky.

It's as if suddenly, without the blanket protection of God, Dad no longer trusts himself.

*

The sour reminder of Dad was not rinsed away by my next long gulp of beer. My thoughts were muddled. What was our quest really about? Was I still hoping to find Dad's redeeming features? Or was I seeking evidence against him to exonerate my sister?

Dad used silence to cover up the truth, but I noted he wasn't entirely selfish. For example, when he died he bequeathed his body to medical research and his eyes to Moorfields Hospital. There was little else of value, only the black metal box. It was tricky to explain why I couldn't throw that away, but I couldn't bring myself to open it either.

After my second strong beer, I was asking myself: why am I reluctant to open the box? Would I find something unwelcome? Might it contradict the version of Dad that I broadcast in his eulogy? But what if by giving me the box, Dad was finally answering my questions and filling in the blanks? Was that possible? Yes. Likely? No.

After Dad's funeral, when I got the box home I grabbed the family photos lying on top, then closed it immediately, rather than go through the old diaries stacked inside. When I consulted friends about the diaries in the attic, they said they would not hesitate to read their deceased Dad's diaries. But they didn't know my Dad, and I feared his viewpoint on those family years would be confronting and uncomfortable.

What I could no longer ignore, as I sat on the terrace in Kenya, was that the box, after its fifteen-year exile in a dark attic, was moving back to centre stage. We had nowhere else to go. We had run out of people to ask, and the new evidence we needed could be right there under our noses. We had lies to overturn.

So, boozed up and alone, I spoke out my decision to the Nairobi night: *'I will open the box!'* This brought an instant sense of relief, as if a spell had been broken.

The next morning, I arrived home from Heathrow, clear-headed and ready. I dropped my bag in the hall, went upstairs and lowered the loft hatch. As I climbed the creaky metal ladder, I made a promise not to fall for any lies Dad had left in his diaries: we would scrutinise and double-check everything.

I put on the light and crawled across the dusty chipboard floor towards the black trunk. It was roughly two feet by one, metal and battered perhaps from military service. There were arcs scratched in the paint beneath the hasp, and a loopy brass handle at either end. In my childhood home, I once found it hidden under a makeshift yellow cover, serving as my parents' bedside table. I never knew what was inside, nor even suspected Dad wrote any diaries.

I lifted the lid cautiously, as if opening a coffin. My hand slipped and the heavy metal lid slammed shut, giving one final chance to walk away. But I took a deep breath, adjusted my squatting position, and raised the lid again to inspect the colourful muddle of old books.

Pulling out one book after another, I spread them out on the floor. There were forty. I arranged them by year: 1944 to 1983. This was a feast of evidence. The red leatherette one had "1971" embossed in gold. Its front cover was sticky (some kind of glue?) and the rear cover was ripped. I turned to a Tuesday in early September. Yes – it was recorded there: *'Call from hospital, died 7.30am'*. I imagined Dad writing those words about the death of his daughter. How? Filled with sadness. When? Secretly, perhaps late at night? I touched the page and inhaled its musty smell.

Next, I picked up a slim black pocket book with a two-winged logo: "The Air Force Diary 1946". Under "Personal Memoranda", Dad put his RAF number (3033838), PO Bank Book number (New Barnet 14774), his collar size (15$^{1/2}$), hat size (7$^{3/8}$) and shoe size (9). On Tuesday 1st January 1946 he was stationed at W.Kirby and went to Liverpool with *'Toddy'* for *'tea and supper at YMCA'*. They queued for an hour at the cinema before they watched "The Seventh Veil" and "Follow That Woman". The ten o'clock train brought them back to base. Bed 11.30. The next day *'little happened'* and Dad wrote several letters. His writing got worse after the first week but he fully used the two pages available every week to capture solid detail.

By this time, my heart was pumping with anticipation about what was to be revealed, but my knees were aching and the light was dim, so I carefully stacked the diaries in a cardboard archive box, to bring downstairs. We had more than enough to start with, and I left behind a manila file labelled "Divorce" and some personal letters, for later.

# Chapter 10: Taboo

In October 2015, I was peering into Dad's life, still eager to dig out the buried secrets of my childhood, but the sheer volume of information in Dad's box was over-whelming: forty years of diaries, each with up to 365 days of handwritten entries! If the quest was to continue, we needed to overcome certain difficulties.

One difficulty was too many random facts to make sense of. For example, the tatty 1959 Letts pocket diary has the Personal Memoranda page filled in with Dad's blue fountain pen giving his name, our Tonbridge address, and phone number, his National Insurance number, Car Registration number (RD 4482), driving licence number and renewal date (29th April). His TV licence was due on 1st January, and Mum was the person to notify in case of accident, with Grandpa as backup. That was just one page.

On Thursday 1st January 1959, the to-do list was: *'blood donor session'* and *'paint curate's ceiling'*. A visit from Danny and June was postponed due to *'children's bad colds'*. On Saturday 3rd January Mum shopped and Dad cemented the front path.

Interestingly, this part jogged a memory: I was a three year old standing there watching Dad as he dragged and jiggled a wooden bar to level the damp concrete.

But dwelling like this on each detail was hopelessly slow.

Inside the front cover was a code in Dad's hand: *'S = Seat, N = No Seat, (n) = n minutes late, + = seat from Sevenoaks'*. So Dad was doing a survey. The entry on Monday 5th January began with '7.4 N (17mins)', telling us he was on the 7.40am, with no seat and it arrived 17 minutes late. Then he wrote *'Points failure Chelsfield'*, which explained the lateness, and *'Wrote to Mr White the Line Traffic Manager'*. So it was possible to decode. I flicked ahead to find Dad continued this train survey until the end of 1959. It underlined his known passion for railways that caused him to learn all the train times by heart, but so what? This left me scratching my head. Why was Dad really doing the survey? What was really driving him? What did it all mean?

During 1959, the marked increase in his meetings did nothing to explain why Dad attended or what actually occurred. We can detect an unreliable car, a daily commute to London, and Dad's founding a rail users' association, joining the Young Liberals, and getting heavily involved with the church.

Dad's apparently innocent, good citizenship was causing me to leap out of bed early each morning, filled with darker explanations. My days became consumed with checking, and each evening I was testing different theories with Helen, to find what actually stacked up.

Fed up with 1959, I soon picked up another diary: 1965. The change after six years was dramatic. Each 1965 diary page was packed with meetings, crossings-out, corrections squashed between the lines, to-do lists and sketchy notes of what Dad called "missions". Still the diary didn't explain Dad's motives. Perhaps the answers were buried in the thirty-eight unread dairies in front of me, but my spirits sank at the thought of going through them all.

Helen suggested we focus on what actually happened between two significant moments we had already identified: the 1959 Humpback Bridge and the 1972 trip to Germany in the Fiat camper van (that I had tried to discuss with my brothers). Confining ourselves to those thirteen years made the task more manageable.

I started writing up Dad's story. When it felt too personal or difficult, I reminded myself there was a moral point to this, although I couldn't quite put that into words, except to say there were principles at stake. My notebook was all crossings-out and restarts, and a lengthening list of questions. My write-up wasn't coming close to describing how golden my family life once was, or how badly things had actually turned out.

No one wanted to help. Mum's "wonder women" were no longer around, except for an aunt a long way away, whose testimony we doubted. The Boys refused to contribute, and there were internal barriers too, in my head and in my heart. An inner critic told me I was getting this out of proportion, making it too large. I was being egocentric, immodest, ungracious, and worse:  the writing didn't matter because no one was interested anyway.

Writer's Block had never been a problem before, but apparently this story refused to be told. I experimented with disguising the story as fiction and giving the characters false names. When that didn't ring true, I tried switched into the present tense, but nothing I tried really worked.

I was struggling, as if underwater and suffocating, and I needed to swim to the surface.

The Creative Writing class at CityLit in Kingsway became a buoyancy aid. This workshop-style class required us to bring in writing samples and take turns to receive feedback. I read out the story of swimming the estuary and the teacher said it was *'strangely intriguing'*, but the muted response of fellow pupils said something else.

Eagerly, I told them about the diaries I'd inherited, but they threw cold water on this: *'Everyone has similar stories'*, they said. I asked: *'Is there a taboo against writing a family story?'*

Someone said *'water only flows downhill'* and parents should *'never be maligned by their children'*. But no, I thought that isn't always right.

Someone condemned the act of *'stealing from a dead man's diaries'* and this brought nods of agreement. But one lady was shaking her head and I was relieved when she spoke up to say: *'As a writer you permit no privacy to the dead: if they leave diaries you have to read them and in this we are utterly unsentimental. To be a writer means to tell the truth you need to tell'*.

While their arguments reverberated around me, I kept my mouth shut. Silently, I noticed that Dad looked like a culprit who was getting away with something, but I reasoned that if we believe someone is wrongly accused, we must do what's needed to clear their name.

I felt like I was the one in the dock, and my classmates' opposition to this project left me shaky and confused. I stayed behind for a quiet chat with the teacher, and told him this was something I really needed to write, even if the class didn't agree. I'd read five of the forty diaries, but he said the diaries weren't written to me, so they weren't speaking to me. That made sense. He said they were probably random notes from a far-too-busy man. Dad's diary said a lot about Dad, but little about me. He said: *'You are looking for your story, not your Dad's story. It is time to start listening to yourself'*.

At the teacher's suggestion, I took a stab there and then: *'I am the son of two parents who wiped a dirty slate clean to give their children a fresh start. But what the parents refused to pass on festered and poisoned our family life. It fell to the son to blow in some fresh air'*.

From that moment, my path began to clear. I was digging out the truth for a reason. The justification came like this: the point to the story is a son sees his father changing. The father is a psychologist getting to grips with questions about human potential: how we can be at our best, at our most productive, fulfilled and happy? But ironically the father becomes caught in a cult that clouds his judgement, making him miserable and destroying his family. The story raises questions for the son on behalf of us all, about how we can escape a century of narcissism which, despite our best intentions, entraps us. We are caused to reflect on how does a human being work, who we are and who we can be.

Suddenly I felt better, but  the teacher's solemn air was a caution. He said that despite the obvious difficulties ahead, I should go down this path, freeing myself up to write, using all available literary means to say what needs to be said.

Over three terms and a summer school, one year in total, I learnt about creative writing in practice, through trying out and polishing more chapters every week. I learned that writing can be play, and entertainment. It can be making sense out of something baffling.

Each chapter I read to the class for the rest of that year was a further surprise. The feedback wasn't ever as expected, and I digested it as best I could on the way home. I was learning how to shine a light on the truth, despite the sometimes deflating scepticism surrounding this project.

When overwhelmed with events and dates and people and links, I borrowed a method from Hilary Mantel's historical research. You write an index card for each character, listing the events they have a hand in. You write cards for each main event, listing the characters involved, and you add what triggers the event and what happens next. You arrange the event cards in date order, you notice when the story shifts and you record how the characters are changed by events.

All sorts of devices became available. Characters can be made to speak to each another, displaying their emotions and letting their dialogue propel the known story events. There are no firm rules. People can travel in time. We can bring in wizards and witches, forces of nature and the magic of dreams. We can shift the point of view, to enlarge the readers' understanding. The narrator can hold everything together by being omniscient, or be given a limited view, and even be made unreliable.

For a memoir, there are tighter limits to creativity. Certain small details are embellished to draw in the reader, but you have to stick to known facts if you want the reader to trust you. You tell the truth as you know it factually, and also as you feel it in your bones. This raises tricky questions. Can you remove a character? Yes, I was told, don't have too many, and focus on a few central people. Can you change a character's name? Yes, for example, if that lets you write the truth without the fear of reprisals. Can you introduce an extra character? Perhaps, but why would you need to?

The writing course extended my creative licence, and set some sensible boundaries. I discovered this wasn't only a story about me, but about fathers, families and society. Briefly, I fancied myself an anthropologist, like Margaret Mead long ago in Samoa, observing a tribe, making ethnographic observations of a culture that were once considered objective. But such observations can never be objective, and the newer practice of "auto-ethnography", allows the writer, by including their own feelings and reflections, to bring about wider changes, both inside themselves, and in the tribe. This brought me hope.

After completing the writing class, I began collecting the arguments for and against proceeding with this story. Historically, fathers were never to be exposed as fallible and human by their sons. Since the Greeks and Romans, fathers were made into saints, for reasons of love, grief or family aggrandisement. For a son to do otherwise, was to sit in judgement. In 1907 Edmund Gosse, an experienced biographer, broke that taboo and dared to write a critical memoir, "Father and Son", which cast his father in a less flattering light. Gosse said the pressure of Victorian formality was creating a *'repression that amounts to death'*. He threw off a *'yoke of dedication'* to *'fashion his inner life for himself'*. I could agree with that.

Gosse received warm letters of praise for the work. Henry James read with *'deep entrancement'*. Rudyard Kipling found the work *'extraordinarily interesting' 'because it's true'*. George Bernard Shaw returned to the book a second time many years after first reading it: *'This was the test, for I could not lay it down until I had been right through it again'*.

Andre Gerard identified this new critical mode of father-memoir and called it "patremoir". He explained how it works. The writer uses their father *'...as raw material for constructing a separate self. It's all about how we create ourselves'*. He traced a line running through Siegfried Sassoon, Evelyn Waugh to later writers and back to Edmund Gosse who was the first author in the sub-genre of "patremoir". This should not be confused with the steady increase in father-son books with which ageing baby boomers seek to immortalise themselves, or cash-hungry writers pander to their readers' sordid appetites for misery.

With this in mind, I re-examined my own motives. I wasn't after producing any great work of literature, just something true. I wasn't chasing celebrity for Dad, the family or myself, and anonymity felt a lot easier, but feedback from my class told me to throw off the disguises and come out into the open: use the real names, tell it in the first person, own my story. As I listened to them, the disguises I employed began to appear as unhelpful and paralysing as the silences of my youth.

Silence denies us understanding, while truth lets us live and breathe.

Gerard said Patremoir is about exploring the relationship of father and son, and also the place and contribution of self in society, letting us raise social concerns such as abusive behaviour, disease, ageing and war. This spoke to my purpose, and emboldened me to stand against the taboo arising in my family and in my writing class that I found so inhibiting and harmful.

I reasoned that if a taboo exists to protect a tribe from threat, it makes sense to cast out the murderers, spies, deadweights, madmen and liars, but not to suppress legitimate social concerns or to silence the tellers of truth.

Each child must learn to live through character-forming events arising out of a complex web of inter-connections in their family, their tribe and the surrounding world. When stuff happens, why would you deprive a child of an understanding that can strengthen them as a person and as a contributor to the tribe? Doesn't every child deserve honesty? If a parent agrees with that, why will they be silent? Truth in our communication strengthens our children, just as lies weaken not only the individuals but also the tribe. When we can embrace our experience for what it is, then we put down roots that strengthen all future decisions and actions.

Such justifications for this project rumbled on inside me. People will benefit. Sharing rather than withholding contributes to a fairer and stronger society. If we can understand who we are to one another, and who we can be, we help remove doubt, shame and resentment. Why not clear away the accretion of superstition, and be undeterred by the out-dated taboos?

So I came to this decision: I will not be shy of delivering a story that can add to the sum total of understanding and empathy and justice and strength in the world. In truth, I have reasons closer to home: family and self. I need to write this for my own sanity, and I don't want my children to be doubtful about their roots either.

I turn a blind eye to those who uphold the taboo, although I continue to ask how far is it fair to go in exploring a father's weaknesses? Incidentally, I've been kind for decades, declaring an admiration for Dad that is only partially true, because it skirts round my confusion and bitter disappointment. I won't make the issue too large: it isn't about murder or sexual abuse, but the time has come to shine a spotlight on my long-dead, and in an all-too-real sense un-dead parents, who have denied me what I hunger for: the truth of my upbringing. Perhaps they had good reasons, or they couldn't help themselves, but I am now willing to risk appearing ungrateful and even unkind, because I am still suffering the consequences: bitter confusion.

Balance and determination will both be needed. A critical survey can demolish the lie and the myths, and I will not gloss over the happy times either:  give merit where it is due. Even when the quest becomes uncomfortable, I'll not be deterred from digging out the evidence and writing down the truth.

This will be worth it if it reduces the bitterness that my "admiration" has failed to disguise. I hope for a verdict other than Dad's guilt and I long for a renewal in family relations built on acceptance rather than denial of what occurred long ago. I want to provoke forgiveness, letting all of us rest in peace, but I don't honestly expect it.

*

This was how I set myself on the path to follow an untold story, wherever it carried me.

In March 2017, I went back to The Boys to tell them the story I'd finally pieced together. After the year of the writing class and nine months coming clean and removing all attempts at anonymity, I'd finished the tenth draft in which my older self was a fly on the wall narrator, following the younger me.

Both meetings started with frosty apprehension and a tightness in my throat, as I began to tell a stiff-faced brother about the secrets inside the box of diaries, and how Helen and I had retraced some childhood footsteps. I don't know if the thawing began in me or my brothers, but their evident interest relaxed me. For a few precious minutes, we cast a light on Dad's part in our childhood, and something was restored: we were close again.

One brother remembered the Deben estuary event: *'After that swim, I could never rely on anyone else'*. That apparently bleak remark was to me a lovely affirmation that the swim happened and it brought us up against the same challenge. Inwardly I began to glow.

Then I put a crucial question: *'Do you want to read the story before it gets published?'* My brother replied: *'No, this old stuff no longer bothers me. I'll just be happy to read it when it comes out'*.

The other brother responded more cautiously: *'What will be in the story?'* I said: *'It isn't about us, but it doesn't reflect too badly on us. And it isn't about now. It's in the past during our early family life. It's about Dad and my story of coming to terms with all of it'*.

I painted the picture of a son, with eyes glued onto a father who was walking away as if to a shining castle on a distant hill. The son yearned for the father to stop and look back, if only to wave, but the father didn't. The son yearned to tag along with his father, but couldn't. In later life, the grown-up son was driven to find out what, long ago, his father found so entrancing.

My brother heard those two stories running side by side and separated by decades. The father's story was in the Sixties: his quest to let human beings grow to their greater potential. Mine is the son's story, signing up to the father's ideal, but horrified at the father's scant regard for family members and the consequent mayhem. The father's legacy is a set of lessons about the distortions of myopia, hypocrisy and fear, and the unintended consequences that arise when a noble intention is pursued.

With this explanation my brother relaxed and smiled: *'Maybe I'll learn something'*.

I came away with more work to do on the draft but, in their contrasting ways, the two brothers who could have halted this project had given me the clearance to proceed.

# Part Three:
## Twenty Wasted Years?

## Chapter 11: Sunny Jim

During October 2015, the writing class buoyed me up and provided the strength to advance. It was five months after my sixtieth birthday, and I remember the clocks were about to change. One morning, sunlight at the window sent me into a dreamy doze and golden ripples illuminated a family surrounding me. Past generations floated like ghosts behind, and future generations kept appearing in front, like waves rolling constantly forwards to the distant horizon.

The next scene zoomed in on babies, those who arrived before me, with laughter and dusty yellow sunbeams. Their childhoods passed quickly without extraordinary events, or puzzles to solve. Then in adulthood, my happy times with Helen arrived, and a cycle repeated in the vivid presence of our children, while our parents were ageing and becoming ghostly shadows in the background. Then we ourselves began fading.

Half-awake, I was pondering how the spirits of ancestors carry on through children and children's children, in a kind of afterlife. We're an entire species, "Homo Sapiens" who have a unique gift that separates us from all others: to choose our behaviour. But is it just an illusion?

The jury's out, I thought.

I got out of bed and returned with two steaming cups of coffee. When Helen sat up to drink one, we ran back over what the quest was showing us.

*

As he approaches the summer of 1969, Sunny Jim, who has for years been walking in sunshine, is starting to feel bored. The trouble is nameless until he expresses his feeling: *'an adventure would be nice'*.

The Deben Estuary provides Sunny Jim's longed for adventure, after which everything will be different for ever. The four swimmers reach the other side, despite the challenges. But the silence says something went terribly wrong. Sunny Jim doesn't know what that could be, and no one's saying.

Sunny Jim is half paralysed in that not knowing.

September arrives and they go back to school.

One day Mum is cooking tea as usual but Dad hasn't come home. When she brings out the food, Sunny Jim sees the red round her eyes. She blurts out: *'Twenty wasted years!'*
No one says anything.

*

Forty-six years later in 2015, we are flies on the wall, drinking coffee and seeing the reason for Mum's upset: this was the day Dad forgot their wedding anniversary. They should have been marking twenty years of marriage, but the extraordinary estuary events made celebrations inappropriate.

*

The creative writing teacher drummed into his class a principle: Show Don't Tell. He once criticised my writing: *'It's as if you're watching a movie in your head and you already know what's going on, but remember we can't see the movie'.* He wanted me to Show, and by that he meant stage the action dramatically, make the point visible to the reader, show the angry man bang a door or thump the table.

This taught me I needed to be a theatre director to bring this story to life. I needed a rule of thumb: have the actors express themselves, speak out and demonstrate what they feel. Where necessary, have them exaggerate, with tears and histrionics, until what they are experiencing becomes vivid and unmistakable, even to a small child.

# Chapter 12: Fun (Dad #1)

During November 2015, I finished reading all Dad's diaries. I wanted to answer a question: was Mum right about "twenty wasted years"? Naturally I was hoping she was wrong. The diaries had shown us four turning points when Dad's character shifted. In order to describe these four changes clearly, I was casting myself as the theatre director. With Helen's help I would extract the story from my head, putting it into a form that is readily understandable to others.

The first of these four phases began after my parents' wedding.

We had an index card for this phase and for the other three turning points, containing cross references to other cards capturing further details of dates, events and the characters. The sources for this information included photographs, letters, diaries, recollections and visits, some of which I have yet to describe. I also had the diaries to hand, if necessary to check, by going through one day at a time, how a particular action developed.

*

- **Settings:** 1949-1959. Clapham. Maidenhead. Bourne End. Train to London. Uganda. Tonbridge.
- **Props:** Fruit bowl. Chopping board. Record Player. Hundreds of photographs of women. Two letters from Africa. Sofa. Cuckoo clock.
- **Characters:** Mummy. Daddy. Auntie M and Auntie G. Uncle R. Sunny Jim. Brothers and sister. Dad's parents. Granny.

Sunny Jim is a twinkle in his parents' eyes when they return from a short honeymoon in the West Country to their Clapham flat in September 1949, as yet unconceived, but faintly imagined as one of four intended children in a five-year plan.

The plan is drawn up during the engagement of a young couple who have no precedent for what they are embarking on: a dual career marriage. They want to be trailblazers in a new era of equality, committed to share the housework and the major decisions. Dad will provide the income, while Mum completes her studies to be a GP. They will move out of London just in time to start the family.

After the honeymoon, they start following the plan. From their flat in Clapham, Mum travels to London Bridge for medical school, while Dad goes to work in Wembley. Dad's sister visits frequently, to find Dad sweeping the floor, or cutting up a fruit salad for the evening meal he is preparing for Mum when she returns. Money is tight. In the evenings, the young couple play 78 rpm records and on special occasions they eat chocolates. Dad goes to church, does the chores, polishes the floorboards, and prepares the evening meals. His sister admires him for this.

But Mum's sister Auntie G soon forms a different impression of Dad.

When Dad finds a job at Southern Electricity Board, the couple move out to a flat at Thicket Corner in Maidenhead, and Mum continues commuting to London Bridge. Living and working in Maidenhead, Dad has time on his hands, and he is bored.  At weekends, he tries to persuade Mum to play mixed doubles at tennis or a game of bridge. He doesn't always succeed, and Mum says it is only common sense for her to study hard, in order to pass her exams.

Auntie G notices a heavy responsibility lands on Mum's shoulders, while Dad occupies himself with all manner of *'extra-curricular activities'*, with the church and all its various clubs. On top of failing to share the chores, Dad neglects Mum too. Yet despite this, Mum giggles with pleasure at every little thing Dad says.

The incident we've already reported, with Dad's brother Uncle R and *'hundreds of photographs of women'*, is just one instance when Dad loses his way. Mum learns to point out Dad's errors gently, not to upset him, and she helps him explore the likely consequences for others whose feelings have been trampled on. Dad promises to be more thoughtful, but he is prone to eagerness and easily forgets these promises. As Dad continues to lose his way, Mum continues to be understanding, while others, including Auntie G, say Mum is becoming *'over-tolerant'*.

In addition to being bored, Dad starts to feel irritated and neglected by Mum, who is often absorbed in her studies. He wants his own behaviour to be beyond reproach, and the local activities allow him a happy escape from Mum's criticism.

Mum passes her finals in the summer of 1953, and in December their daughter is born. In 1954, the couple raises a mortgage on a shabby terrace house in the nearby village of Bourne End. Everything is just about going according to plan.

One more scene illustrates their relationship in this phase. Two letters arrive in March 1954 from the two sisters in Africa. The first letter, from Mum's sister Auntie G in Nairobi, recounts a serious flying accident on the way to a wedding in Uganda, which puts Auntie G and her husband Uncle T in hospital. The second letter, from Dad's sister Auntie M in Uganda, tells of a disastrous flying accident the day before her wedding, causing her dress, the cake, the chief bridesmaid (Auntie G) and the man giving her away (Uncle T), never to arrive. Auntie M tells how she put on a stiff upper lip and went ahead anyway, so all was well in the end.

Dad writes back to *'admonish'* his sister for her thoughtlessness. He demands she apologise to Mum's sister, who might have died in the plane crash. Auntie M, aggrieved at her brother's *'high moral tone'*, protests this was her wedding day and she did nothing wrong. Despite her reservations, she makes earnest attempts to reach out to Auntie G, but is rebuffed each time. Mum apologises to everyone and regrets her part in this misunderstanding although, it is obvious to anyone, this was Dad's doing. After the rebuke, Dad's sister admires Dad less. Curiously, it turns out that two aunts, once firm friends, never speak to one another again.

Sunny Jim is born into this family in 1955, to live with his Mummy and Daddy and a sister who arrived seventeen months earlier. His two younger brothers then follow in quick succession. This is the happy mini-world of Sunny Jim's childhood. The workload of childcare and housework is largely invisible to everyone except Mummy, because she takes care of it all.

Daddy becomes the master of fun. It suits him. Sunny Jim climbs over him on the sofa, sits on his shoulders and rubs his sandpaper chin. On special occasions, Daddy provides the party games. The children bury him in the sand at the beach. He is there for the excitement, not for the housework.

When Daddy's parents come to visit, they are cross about something. Mummy looks tired and anxious, saying Daddy's family have *'impossibly high standards'*. Despite the demands on her, Sunny Jim can still rely on the cuddles and stories at bedtime.

In 1957, soon after Daddy's job moves to the National Coal Board in London, the family home moves to Tonbridge in Kent, where Mummy finds a part-time position as a GP.

In August 1959, during the Humpback Bridge incident, Sunny Jim is laughing so much with Daddy that he hardly notices Mummy's reaction. But when Daddy is put in charge, Sunny Jim often ends up crying, because Daddy finds it impossible to cope simultaneously with four young ones. During these disasters, Sunny Jim misses Mummy.

Sunny Jim gets used to not seeing Daddy in the evening, because the trains are running late. Daddy sets up a Rail

Travellers Association. He immerses himself in politics, and campaigns for the The Liberals to win the general election. He attends a local evangelical centre at Hildenburgh Hall with its religious talks, and he sets up a Parish Action Group to restore the decaying local church. Daddy buys a car, and its frequent breakdowns add to the unpredictability of his departures and arrivals.

Daddy has a cunning plan to get an extra pair of hands at home. He says it's a brilliant creative solution, but Sunny Jim never expects Granny to move in, until she does. Mummy doesn't want her mother anywhere near but, despite this opposition, it happens anyway.

Sunny Jim enjoys the treat of watching the TV in Granny's bedroom. There are two armchairs, and a budgie cage hanging from a high chrome stand, and he laughs every fifteen minutes when the cuckoo pops out of the clock.

Granny offers Sunny Jim tea in a china cup, with yellow and pink Battenberg cake. When he says: *'Yes please!'* Granny says: *'What did your last servant die of?'* When Granny talks about the hunt for her missing husband, who was shell-shocked after the war, she says the police dredged the River Thames.

Sunny Jim asks: *'How old was Mummy when her daddy went missing?'*
Granny answers: *'Five'.*

Sunny Jim is also five, and can't imagine being without a daddy. Life would be much less fun.

Granny sings *'It's a Long Way to Tipperary...'* while she bathes the children, and the words make Sunny Jim wonder if Granny thinks bedtime is a long way away.

*

As theatre director, I staged those scenes in November 2015, allowing me to live through Sunny Jim's first five years. I felt the young boy's excitement, as part of the family, swept along as part of a little crowd. I got to like the Fun Daddy, whose shortcomings were invisible to Sunny Jim, but far plainer to his mother. I wondered which parent was really the one with the problem. Sunny Jim had no idea that his parents were torn apart between their plan and the reality of their lives as husband and wife. A problem was developing between them, and both parents bore some responsibility.

While I was staging Sunny Jim's life, I felt excited like a young boy. But each time I took a break and walked past the mirror in the hall, I glimpsed my lined face, and wondered where the young boy had gone.

Let me describe the method by which those scenes were created. I'd cleared our oak dining table and turned it sideways, as we do when we have guests, to give them space. The end closest to the easy chairs was covered in a tea towel: this defined the stage.

Next, as theatre director I figured out who was to appear the first scene. I imagined the flat in Clapham, then placed objects, such as an apple or a teacup (there was no particular symbolism in the object), on the "stage" to represent each character, in this case Dad and Auntie M, paying attention to where they would be standing and which way they faced. Each scene, including the one with Granny, was set like this. I used small paper labels to represent the essential props, such as armchairs, the budgie cage, cuckoo clock and TV.

I imagined the audience in the easy chairs watching that stage. There was a good deal of trial and error. After roughing out a scene, I talked Helen through it, because she has the knack for noticing how the characters can excite or grate on one another. Together we challenged every move and walked through the alternatives, until finally I settled on the truth of it. So the story advanced, often with a realistic dialogue to propel the drama.

Once sense-tested, I wrote it all down, putting Sunny Jim's experience into the present tense, as if it was happening now and for the very first time. My narrator voice described what Sunny Jim saw, felt and heard, what he said or did about it and what the other characters said or did in response.

# Chapter 13: Strict (Dad #2)

It was December 2015. I was re-setting the dining table stage to depict the Sixties, with Sunny Jim in his sheltered life and blind to events in the wider world.

I walked round the table, with a make-believe camera to catch different angles and viewpoints, and fantasised that I was making an engrossing movie. All kinds of near-to-hand objects represented my family members. On a whim I used grapes, apples, chewing gum tablets, eggs, drip mats, glasses and USB sticks to stand in for them.

It was becoming obvious that Daddy was starting to change.

*

- **Settings:** 1960-1965. The Boys' bedroom. Vegetable garden. Church Nativity Play. New curate's class. TV studio.  Greenhouse. Bushy Park
- **Props:** TV set with news headlines. 3 beds. Green Hillman. Spade. "Honest to God" book. Election flyer. Municipal diary. Social Survey report. Beatles concert poster.  Empty cardboard box.
- **Characters:** The family. Granny. New curate. Auntie M. Helen.

Sunny Jim is five years old when a new decade begins: The Sixties, famous for sex and drugs and rock'n roll. But no one at home knows or cares about what's changing in the world, except for Daddy.

The world is not as Daddy believes it ought to be, and it's worse than that: the world is moving in totally the wrong direction, towards the immoral. Examples include the Lady Chatterley Trial, the Pill, Abortion, Divorce, Cuban Missiles, Communism, Vietnam and the Cold War.

Some say it is a great time to be a man, such as young John F Kennedy, until he dies in November 1963 on the eve of greatness. But it's not a great time to be Daddy because his beloved railways are savagely cut in the Beeching Report of

1963. His Liberal party comes a poor third in the general election of 1964. The Profumo scandal featuring a government minister and a sexual relationship with a would-be model only confirm the general public's preference to be titillated by the doings of celebrities, rather than play their part in the serious business of governing and improving society.

The early years go by in a blur, because the four children are young and easily amused by games no more complicated that folding newspapers to make party hats, but these games are happening less often because Daddy is becoming busier.

Early in 1962, the family home moves from Tonbridge to Maidstone, and this gives Mummy further to drive to work. The children have to move schools, and Granny is unhappy too. Dad's job is the reason: he moves to Reed Paper Group in Maidstone.

Sunny Jim's bedroom contains three beds in a line with a young boy in each. On evening at bedtime Daddy walks in and shows The Boys the trick of locking their left and right knuckles together, then raising a steeple with the two fore-fingers while reciting: *'Here's a church, here's a steeple',* then he twists his hands over and wiggles the fingertips inside, *'and there's the people'.*

This produces many attempts to copy, and lots of laughter, before Daddy's next move: *'It is time to teach you how we pray silently to God up in heaven'.*

Then the laughter is over, and the three boys kneel at their beds, putting hands flat together and closing their eyes. Daddy says: *'What we have to do is, remember exactly what happened today. God already knows everything we are seeing and thinking, so we can ask for help silently in our heads'.*

Daddy doesn't notice Sunny Jim squint covertly at two obedient brothers. He continues: *'If something good happened today, then thank God silently. Now remember what you did wrong today, and ask God to forgive these sins'.*

Time drags in the silence, until a closing phase: *'You go through the family one by one, and ask God to give them whatever they need. Last of all you ask God for anything you need. Remember, God doesn't like boys who are selfish and he won't give you what you ask for, unless you're also helping everyone else'.*

It is a lot for small boys to take in. But Sunny Jim reckons God probably knows him in much the same as Daddy and Mummy, who mostly know what he's thinking.

When they open their eyes, Daddy is smiling and he says: *'Good people go to church and say their prayers'*, and *'we must all be well-behaved because only the good ones go to heaven'.* Sunny Jim is learning that God has a divine plan for everyone, and the hand of God is in every lucky event, and by praying you find out about miracles like when the cat goes missing and then a neighbour offers a guinea pig as a replacement, and when the get home after a long journey home, without crashes.

Sunny Jim tells Daddy he prayed for Mummy to tuck them in. Daddy promises to ask her but says it is too late for stories. He turns out the light and leaves.

A few minutes later Mummy comes in and Sunny Jim asks her if all the children in the world actually say their prayers. She says: *'Only the good ones'*, but Sunny Jim doubts that's really true.

Daddy is becoming much less fun. He writes out the weekly rota of chores and puts the children's names in the boxes for daily washing up, putting away, getting coal, and the weekly car washing. There is a strict weekly food routine: roast dinner on Sunday, cold meat on Monday, mince or shepherd's pie on Tuesday, bubble and squeak or macaroni cheese on Wednesday, toad in the hole on Thursday, yellow smoked haddock poached in milk on Friday,  and spam or luncheon meat salad on Saturday.

When Sunny Jim helps dig the vegetables, Daddy grabs the spade: *'Not like that!'*, Sunny Jim watches Daddy do it "properly". Daddy looks frenzied and quite alone.

Church is an obsession. It happens three times every Sunday, grace is said before the meals, and prayers before bed. Sister goes to Sunday School. The Boys are taught by Daddy to sing, and this earns them places in the choir. Daddy gives away the green Hillman Husky (JJG 563) to the new curate, making a big show of generosity. Mummy doesn't approve.

On Sundays, Sunny Jim looks across towards the men in the church choir, but Daddy isn't always there and he wonders what Daddy is getting up to instead.

One day, The Boys are in trouble because money is missing from Mummy's purse. That night at bedtime, Daddy smacks them five times on their bare bottoms, but Sunny Jim gets five extra smacks for "telling tales" because he confessed during Daddy's fierce questioning. Telling-the-truth is apparently required, but telling-tales isn't, and that's puzzling. So when The Boys get punished again for buying cigarettes, instead of confessing again, Sunny Jim keeps quiet.

It is coming up to Christmas in 1963. At bedtime prayers, Daddy tells The Boys about the new curate putting on a Nativity Play at church. Everyone is talking about what happened. The play starts normally, with mother Mary, baby Jesus, the angels and shepherds, until Teddy Boys barge in, and kick over the crib. There is a fight and the police are called. In the midst of the mayhem, the curate stands up waving his arms to settle everyone. They know it's a set-up when he asks: *'How would you like to the play to end?'*

Dad tells The Boys he stayed behind to chat with the curate, while the rest of the congregation left grumbling. Dad signed up for a weekly class run by the curate where they studied a book called "Honest to God". This book proves heaven and hell do not actually exist after all. God is not a white-robed man in the clouds: He is inside us. It means that when Daddy prays, something different happens because Daddy is listening for the God inside. After this, when Daddy has a creative idea, it is from God so everyone has to obey.

Sunny Jim feels that God and Daddy are getting mixed up.

For several weeks at the class, the curate is asking Daddy the same question: *'How would you like the play to end?'* After four weeks, the answers start arriving in Daddy's mind:

*'My life will be a set of missions: a Sociological one to embrace the poor, a Political one to run the council, a Religious Mission to unite the churches, and an Industrial one to stop the strikes'.*

Sunny Jim finds it impossible to follow, but understands that Daddy no longer helps at home because he is helping in other ways. His strict and absent Daddy is contributing something fantastic and worthwhile, and one day everyone in the wider world will be very grateful.

In May 1964, Daddy is elected a local councillor and this advances his "Political Mission". Mummy's words on the election flyer declare Daddy's *'dedication to helping people is an opportunity for everyone in Maidstone to benefit from his limitless and so far unbridled energy'.*

The Maidstone Municipal Diary has Daddy down for many of the committees: Transport, Traffic, Civic Development, Baths, Parks and Home Safety. He is also a school governor. After work he goes straight to these council meetings. He is dashing everywhere and turning up late.

At the start of 1965, Daddy's "Sociological Mission" springs to life. Mummy joins Daddy's working group with the new curate and a professor from Southampton. Each Sunday evening, they sit in the dining room behind piles of papers, to design questionnaires, and analyse results. Their report, "Maidstone A Closer Look" is published in the summer, followed by TV and radio interviews in the autumn. Sunny Jim doesn't see so much of Daddy or Mummy that year, and they both look tired.

Daddy is not just getting confused about God, but also about right and wrong. During May 1965, Grandma (Daddy's mother) is getting remarried, and Daddy is driving back from the wedding, with his sister beside in the front seat. Sunny Jim is pretending to sleep on the backseat while listening avidly to their raging argument. Daddy does not object to the marriage in principle, but the problem is Grandma marrying Grandpa's brother. Daddy's sister says there is no problem, and no legal impediment, what with Grandpa being dead. In fact, they will both be happier together. But Daddy refuses to accept this. He says it is morally wrong to marry an existing family member, and against God's law.

While arguing, Daddy's driving is terrifying. He throws the car at roundabouts. Sunny Jim can guess Dad's reasons: if God agrees with Dad's argument, they will all be OK. If God doesn't agree, Dad will simply apply the brakes to prevent an accident.

Daddy isn't happy. He is returning late in the evenings, looking tired, complaining about the small-mindedness and complacency of people at the council. As for work, he speaks of being trapped between the vested interests of workers on the left and owners on the right. Those two halves are locked in endless conflict.

One night, Sunny Jim calls from his bed for a story. Mummy replies: *'Not tonight dear. You're too old – and besides, there's far too much to do.'*

*'Will you tuck me in then?'*
*'OK, just coming.'*

As Mummy enters, he gazes at her. Mummy's face softens as she

says: *'Shall I tell you a secret?'*
This is exciting: *'Oh, yes please!'*

*'Tomorrow, we're having a present for the family. I can't tell you what it is yet.'*
*'Please, please, why can't you tell me?'*
*'Then it won't be a surprise.'*

*'Do the others know?'*
*'No, it's just between us: you, me and Daddy.'*
With happy anticipation, Sunny Jim drops off to sleep.

At breakfast, Mummy is frowning. Has she forgotten? Sunny Jim corners her in the kitchen: *'When are we going to have the surprise?'*

*'Not yet dear. Daddy has gone to work and we don't want him to miss it. We'll have to wait until he comes home.'*

With this, all hope collapses, because Daddy is always returning too late. But Daddy comes home on time for a change and wearing the broad grin once so familiar, but now so rare.

He asks everyone to gather at the foot of the stairs, where they sometimes assemble for "family prayers". He makes an announcement: *'This is a family meeting, and we have some good news!'*

Daddy's excitement is reflected in everyone's faces. They have not had a "family meeting" before, and Sunny Jim is sure his promised surprise is about to arrive. Noisily they demand: *'What is it?', 'Tell us what it is', 'Don't leave us in suspense!'*
Daddy releases it: *'I have a new job!'*

Sunny Jim is puzzled. Is this the surprise? Is it a good thing? Has he been tricked?
Daddy just continues beaming.
Mummy steps in to repair things: *'How exciting!'*
Sunny Jim doesn't believe her.

Daddy continues: *'Yes, I am going into a more interesting line of work. It's called management training'.*

Sunny Jim asks grumpily: *'Where is the job?'* He is worried everyone will have to move again.

Daddy replies: *'I am travelling to London instead of working locally'.*
Sunny Jim asks: *'What does this mean for the rest of us?'*

In response, Daddy gives out clipboards, pens and paper: *'That's why I'm giving you something to write on. This job is a sideways move, and travelling to London each day is expensive so we need to economise...'*
He is interrupted: *'What?' 'Sideways move?' 'Economise?'*

Mum translates: *'It means we have to save some money'.*

Someone asks: *'What do we write on the pads?'*
Daddy explains: *'Write down all your ideas to save money. It's called brainstorming'.*

Silence again.
Sunny Jim doesn't want to give up any treats.
No one else is writing either.
Daddy urges them on: *'Come on! Just write down what's not really necessary?'*

Reluctantly they shout out their favourite things: *'Sweets'. 'Toys'. 'Presents'. 'Picnics'. 'Holidays'. ' Ice creams'. 'Custard'. 'Fish and chips'. 'Heating'. 'New clothes'. 'The car'.*

It feels hopeless and wrong to sacrifice their treats for the sake of Daddy's new job and Sunny Jim has a better idea: *'Why don't we bake cakes and sell them? And, what if Mummy works more hours?'* He doesn't notice it's unkind to Mummy.

At bedtime, Mummy finds Sunny Jim sobbing in bed: *'What's the matter dear?'*
Sulkily, he complains: *'Was that supposed to be the secret surprise?'*

*'Oh no, that was something quite different, but the surprise has gone missing.'*
*'What has gone missing?'*

*'A lovely fluffy, white and ginger guinea pig.'*
*'Why can't you find it?'*

*'Well we brought it home last night in a cardboard box, from a*
*neighbour who had too many new babies in the cage…'*
*'How did it get lost?'*

*'We put the box in the greenhouse and this morning it was*
*empty: the guinea pig had vanished.'*

Later that night, Mummy is playing the piano and her sweet
tune dissolves the sourness left over by Daddy's wrong-footing,
Mummy's covering it up, and the guinea pig's mysterious
disappearance.

The next day, Sunny Jim starts to call Daddy by a new grown-up
name: Dad.

*

In December 2015, as theatre director watching these family
events on my dining table stage, I was not unaffected: in fact, I
found it very moving. Sunny Jim hated the family prayers, and
those family meetings, but he was also sad when both family
rituals ended shortly after this, because he wanted the presence
and constancy of Dad.

I researched the "Honest to God" book that so gripped Dad
and his curate. It sold a million copies in seventeen languages.
The author was John Robinson, a radical bishop who wanted to
start a religious revolution, by saying the unsayable. That same
Robinson was called to testify at the Lady Chatterley trial, where
he declared: *'sex is an act of holy communion'*.
By the end of this chapter, I had watched Sunny Jim growing up
towards ten, with life at home getting more serious. He had no
clue why Strict Dad had taken the place of Fun Daddy.

*

Decades after the last scene, we were walking through Bushy
Park holding onto Mum, because she had a tendency to go
walkabout. Our daughter was a toddler, riding on my shoulders,

and our little son was walking beside Helen. At that time, Mum rarely spoke, but her smile made it obvious she loved our small children. I was surprised when she asked: *'How many will you have?'*

Without thinking I said: *'It's impossible to handle more than two'.*

I did not mean it as a criticism but, as the second of her four children I knew she found it hard to cope with us all. It was obvious I'd touched a nerve when Mum's smile disappeared and her eyes welled up. I wanted to bring the smile back to her face and I asked: *'Do you remember the guinea pig?'*

It was improbable because Mum remembered very little by then.

She smiled faintly, but then her reply was surprisingly definite: *'Yes, it was such a pity'.*
This was delightful, and to keep a rare contact going I pressed her: *'So what actually happened?'*

She paused with a concentrated frown, then lightened and answered lucidly: *'The guinea pig drowned in the watering can, but we didn't tell the children in case it upset them'.*

After that fleeting moment, Mum returned to dementia.

## Chapter 14: Crash

It was January 2016. We needed a scene to explain a flip that happened to Dad in 1965, shortly after the visit of Auntie C's family from America.

Helen said: *'What sort of flip?'*
I said: *'His complete change of priorities'.*
She had an idea: *'Maybe if we visit Maidstone?'*
So we paid a visit, to try to explain Dad's flip.

After the ninety-minute swoop round the M25, we drove over the new Medway Bridge that sits alongside the old stone one, and followed the long one-way loop round Maidstone's town centre. Halfway down the busy hill, I was startled by a new red traffic light outside our old house-on-the-corner, because it didn't used to be there. Instead of turning left into King Edward's Road, we were forced straight on, and we needed to take three more left turns before we pulled up beside my old house.

When we got out of the car, I saw the house sepia-tinted and heard white noise behind the faint tinkle of children's laughter. Momentarily, I was enchanted and back in 1965, but the spell broke when I saw the privet hedge overhanging the pavement, the weeds in the garden, the shabby flaking paint on the house, and the overgrown shrubs pressed up to the windows shutting out the light. I walked round the front wall seeking anything familiar. The swing in the front garden was missing, but ahh, another brief flicker of magic, there were the front gateposts!

*

- **Setting:** 1965. Maidstone house at busy road junction.
- **Props:** Gatepost. 3 crashed cars. Apron. Doctor's bag. Police, ambulance and tow truck. Sirens.
- **Characters:** The Boys. Mum.

It's a Friday in July 1965, and it's summer. Sunny Jim in short trousers, with collar open, long sleeves rolled up and hair neatly parted sits on the capping stone of a tall brick gatepost with a notebook and pencil, jotting down the registration numbers of passing cars. At this crossroads, the busy main road has priority. It's a hill, where cars race down from the right towards the town centre, and it's hard to catch their numbers, but easy to catch the slower cars chugging uphill from the left.

Mum's wedding ring tapping the window signals to Sunny Jim it's teatime, so he climbs down from the gatepost ready to go indoors. In that instant, there is a terrible crash with the sound of breaking glass, and a second loud bang. Before he looks, Sunny Jim knows it's bad. He climbs back up: the road is blocked, steam is hissing out and there is blood.

He runs into the house calling: *'Mum!'*
She dashes out with her apron on, and The Boys follow.
She sends them back inside shouting: *'Don't look!'*

Mum follows The Boys inside and dials 999. The Boys, with their noses pressed to the kitchen window, argue excitely about what happened, and whose fault it is. A dark red Jaguar Mark II was racing down the hill, and a grey Morris Minor was in the way, creeping too slowly across from King Edwards Road on the left to Campbell Road opposite. An old black Rover heading up the hill didn't notice, so that was the second bang as it ploughed into the two mangled cars.

Mum, her apron removed and doctor's bag in her right hand, is walking briskly down the path and through the front gate towards a terrible mess. She tends the wounded.

There are sirens and flashing lights. Police and ambulance and tow trucks arrive to take away the bodies and the remains of three cars.

After a very long time, the traffic starts to flow again. Mum returns to face questions from The Boys: *'What happened?"*
*'The red car was driving too fast.'*

*'Was anyone hurt?'*
*'Yes. Two drivers and a passenger. We sent them to hospital.'*
*'What happened to the Jaguar driver?'*
*'He died.'*

*

I told the story of that crash to Helen, because seeing the gatepost brought it flooding back. Our family was like the grey Morris Minor, creeping along happily, and until the crash we had no idea how vulnerable we were.

The visit from the Americans was more complicated to re-member. Helen and I walked down the hill from our house, hoping to trigger something. By this time, Helen's hip was getting better and she welcomed gentle exercise. We turned right opposite All Saints Church, towards the cinema where I once went to see Mary Poppins with the Americans. As we approached, I felt the happy vibe of that day in July 1965 with the film and the ice creams in the company of cousins.

When we reached the cinema, it had morphed into a bingo hall. As we walked back up the hill, I remembered the evening when Uncle J from America rang our doorbell and I was supposed to be asleep in bed.

As I relayed this to Helen, I put Uncle J and Dad on an imagined stage and we played out a series of moves to explain Dad's subsequent flip. The words in the characters' mouths might have been difficult for a ten year old to understand, but the vibe between Uncle J and Dad (they didn't see eye to eye) was unmistakable.

*

- **Settings:** 1965. Maidstone house at busy road junction. Cinema. Dining room. Kitchen.
- **Props:** Piles of papers. Big road map of Maidstone. Cybernetics book.
- **Characters:** The family, Uncle J, Auntie C, 4 American cousins.

It is Saturday, the day after the big car accident in front of Sunny Jim's house. Sunny Jim is looking forward to The Americans' arrival. He sits impatiently inside, peering out through the kitchen window to check the road.

All of a sudden, Mum rushes to the front door and a loud female voice is saying *'Hiiiee'*, *'Wowww'* and *'Gooorrrgeeeoousss'*. No one else speaks so loudly with the vowels so stretched but the words are familiar, and Mum's quiet voice rises a fraction in response.

Sunny Jim sees Auntie C through the kitchen window. She is standing by the open front door in a bright blue and gold dress. Mum wears her usual green slacks and a brown cardigan. They are not obviously sisters. Auntie C is dragging Mum and Dad outside:

*'You guys must come out to the station wagon and meet our guys!'*

The large American "station wagon" is blocking the main road outside. This is a dangerous spot. Cars are already hooting. Uncle J turns left into King Edwards Road and pulls up by the pavement where the family is lined up like a welcoming party.

One by one, four super-sized children unfold themselves from the station wagon onto the pavement. There is a lot of noise. The cousins are sun-tanned and freckly, with sparkling white teeth. The girls have bright dresses and the boys wear denims with check shirts. The oldest girl is seventeen, the fifteen-year-old boy is the tallest, the twelve-year-old girl is skinny like a pencil, and the other boy is younger but far larger than Sunny Jim.

Uncle J steps out last, with white stubble and uncombed grey balding hair, quite unlike Dad who is clean-shaven with black tidy hair, in the white shirt and tie he wears at weekends. Uncle isn't glamorous or smiley, but he is stylish in a different way, with red braces over a pale yellow shirt, a potbelly pushing down the front of his trousers and pointed tan leather cowboy boots.

Instead of blocking the pavement, the six new arrivals are escorted by their six hosts, through the side gate to the lawn. Everyone spreads out on the rugs, and over glasses of orange squash, the Americans talk about their trip.

Uncle stands up to issue an invitation: *'The Yanks would like to invite the Brits to see Mary Poppins at the local movie theatre'*. He speaks in a theatrical, playful way.

Dad makes an acceptance speech in a similar tone, and surrenders the next day, a Sunday normally reserved for church, because for the Americans this is the only possible time.

On Sunday afternoon, the Americans call in for the Brits and the whole group walks happily down the hill to the cinema. The film is wonderful. At the interval, Auntie C laughs: *'On holiday our only rule is wherever we see an ice-cream, we have to buy one!'* Then she buys ice-creams all round.

As they walk back up the hill, the girls with Mum and Auntie C are dawdling at the back. A pack of boys walks ahead. Uncle J and Dad are in the middle of the pack chatting. Sunny Jim walking nearby sees Uncle J do a little dance: *'Hey man, I'm Dick Van Dyke, doing Chim Chimeree like a Brit!'*
Dad smiles faintly: *'Thanks for treating us'.*

Uncle turns to Dad: *'This should help Anglo-American relations: a movie by the American Walt Disney, set in London. I hope we've scored a goal'.*
Dad dislikes boastful talk, but Uncle is only breaking the ice.

Uncle perseveres: *'May I ask you something Mr Page?'*
Dad nods: *'Of course'.*
*'So far today I've seen five near traffic accidents. How do you live with that?'*
*'It's worse than you think. I see the accident reports.'*

Uncle perks up: *'Might we look at this together?'*
Dad accepts: *'Tonight. Our house at eight o'clock?'*

The doorbell rings on the dot of eight, but Mum is out catching up with her sister, Auntie C, at the hotel. Dad opens the front door: *'Hello, do come in. Let's go in here, where we won't be disturbed'.*

Sunny Jim in his pyjamas sees this from the top of the stairs. He tiptoes down and watches the men through the crack in the dining room door. He sees Uncle cast his eye around at piles of papers everywhere from the Social Survey, and a large map spread out on the table: *'I guess this is the life of a busy town councillor'.*

Dad takes him straight to the map: *'All the black crosses are accidents. Just two days ago there was a fatal one right outside. Something has to be done'.*

The men are absorbed. Uncle is pacing up and down: *'Would you describe one of the accidents please?'*
Dad tells him about the red Jaguar coming down the hill, and the grey Morris creeping across. Uncle's mind gets to work and he's firing questions: *'What exactly can the driver see from each car?'*

It's not long before Dad leaps up, and shouts: *'Sunny Jim! Go straight back up to bed, right now!'*
Sunny Jim doesn't dare argue when Dad uses that voice. To prove his obedience he stamps loudly back to bed, then tiptoes back to the top step where an ear pressed to the wood panel picks up every word from below.

Uncle is saying the road is a river and fast, powerful Jaguars are bound to collide with weaker, slower cars downstream. Dad says there are two kinds of trip: the locals and the Londoners.

They go on like this until it's obvious they've solved it, because Uncle bellows in a big delighted voice: *'Why of course! We'll make it one way!'*
Dad says: *'Perfect! Thank you J. I'll take this straight to the Committee!'*

Then Uncle asks a strange question: *'I'm curious about everything you're taking on here Mr Page. Could you explain what drives you?'*
*'It's late'* is how Dad replies, then their chairs grate on the parquet floor, and Sunny Jim dashes back into bed.

The following night, Mum goes out again to meet Auntie C, and at eight o'clock the doorbell rings. Dad answers. It is Uncle J again and they resume where they left off, with Sunny Jim listening in just like before.

Dad is answering Uncle's parting question: *'What drives me? Winning the election is one thing: It's like being chosen. You will understand that if you are a religious man'.*

Uncle doesn't reply for a long time, which means he doesn't get it, but Dad continues eagerly describing his religion and his "missions", like he's trying to save the world.

Then Uncle says: *'So the folks at home won't see that much of you'.* And he moves to a different topic: *'Now can I tell you what drives me?'*

Their voices are hushed then, until Uncle says: *'Let me ask you straight. Why are you fiddling with traffic lights? And all this local church business. Don't you see the larger game?'*

Uncle describes the game like Sunny Jim's sports teacher: *'You're just doing the tiny things, instead of facing the real enemy whose missiles are ready to wipe you out!'* Uncle drops Cuba into the conversation and the Russians: *'Moscow's just a short hop, but what are you Brits doing about it? Fiddling is all you're doing!'*

Dad gets angry. Sunny Jim can't see his face from the top of the stairs, but hears the outburst: *'You're putting us in harm's way, while The Americans are hiding in safety six thousand miles away!'*
Uncle tries to calm him: *'Look don't worry. You're all totally safe. Mutually Assured Destruction takes care of that'.*

Dad stays silent, until Uncle backs down: *'OK, OK, you're right. Mutually Assured Destruction is despicable! But we do have an alternative'.* Uncle outlines his better idea: *'Confidentially, we have even more back up. We will soon have the means to build human colonies under the sea, and in outer space too. If nuclear war makes it uninhabitable, that's how we'll survive'.*

Dad starts to shout: *'You can't be serious J, that is no kind of a life!'* And Sunny Jim understands that the world might be destroyed.

The screech of chairs on the parquet warns Sunny Jim to dive into bed. From his pillow, he hears the front door close as Uncle J departs.

The next morning Sunny Jim comes down early to ask Mum:

*'Will the Russians send missiles to blow everyone up?'*
Mum stops laying the table and looks at him: *'Of course not
Sunny Jim, whoever put that idea in your head?'*

\*

After our trip to Maidstone in January 2016, Helen and I
returned home to South West London, and by then we had
sense-tested the story. Yes, the crashes actually happened, The
Americans actually visited and a switch flipped in Dad's head.

Uncle J was our perfect way of explaining the change in Dad.
We checked the Internet for details of the part Uncle J played in
the Cold War as a rocket scientist, and these matched up with
what had been passed on by Auntie C and her daughter, Cousin
M. After meeting and marrying Auntie C over here in the UK,
Uncle J's war ended and the couple returned to the US, where
he worked with the US Navy on anti-aircraft guns and missile
defence. In the years that followed, Uncle J published scientific
papers and was one of 59 people invited to a Macy Conference
*'to set the foundations for a general science of the workings
of the human mind'.* They're all named in the Wikipedia entry:
eminent professors and scientists from across the US including
the anthropologist Margaret Mead, and one W. Ross Ashby who
was a founder of the new subject of Cybernetics. That Uncle J's
personal project was investigating how to support human life
after a nuclear war, was verified in 1980 when we visited Auntie
C on our honeymoon.

Uncle J and Dad were a couple of scientists drawn to solve the
physical problem of traffic accidents in Maidstone. But their
profound differences over religion and the Cold War drove them
apart. When we picked up Dad's box after the funeral, the book
"An Introduction to Cybernetics" by W Ross Ashby (1956) was
amongst those things, but it was brand new and unopened, most
likely a gift from Uncle J, to prove some obscure point they had
been discussing, or perhaps to say no hard feelings.

For Dad, the meeting with Uncle J was like meeting the devil,
and having his faith tested. In a photo taken at Heathrow the day
the Americans flew home, Dad looked miserable and defeated.
Sunny Jim was miserable for a different reason: he would miss

The Americans, and their happy, laid-back life.

Soon after the Americans went home, Dad's spirit returned as he rearranged his priorities. He flipped from being a strict defender of the status quo, to being a fighter for change. Instead of ditching his "missions" as Uncle J advised, progress became more urgent. Dad said the purpose was to bring about a "perfect mini-society", as if this could reduce the probability of nuclear annihilation.

Later on, Mum called Dad's ambitions *'grandiose'* and *'cruel'*, and *'no better than Uncle J'*. She said Dad was seduced by *'utopian dreams'*, and the *'hysteria of crowds'*. She mentioned Aldous Huxley, and said Dad was putting *'ends before means'*, because his chosen "means" would fail to reach the "ends" he was seeking: *'Hitler and every other war in human history taught us that!'* With such intellectual arguments, Mum took the wind out of Dad's sails.

Helen and I sat at the dining table going over the whole story, satisfied with our explanation for Dad's flip, until she threw in a complete wobbler: *'Did your Dad have the hots for Auntie C?'*

I couldn't answer that.

# Chapter 15: Hippie (Dad #3) and the Hammer Blows

It was February 2016. As theatre director, I was re-experiencing Sunny Jim's early life from every possible angle, and it was insightful. By the age of ten, Sunny Jim's life had fallen into two distinct halves: with Fun Daddy up to five years old, and with Strict Dad thereafter. I saw Sunny Jim trying to be quiet and well-behaved, to please rather than anger his father. This failed as a strategy because the child became invisible, and easier for his father to ignore. The small child, who looked to Dad's presence for his happiness, had difficulty accepting that Dad had found something else more attractive.

During the next five years, the pace of Dad's life only increased, and with this Sunny Jim's need to understand what was driving his Dad away.

*

- **Settings:** 1966 – 1970. Maidstone. Rochester under the floorboards. Beach. Polytechnic.
- **Props:** Razor. Dad's new clothes. TV news. Movie camera. Cricket. Wires and tools. Vauxhall. Cortina.
- **Characters:** Dad. Waifs and strays.

Hippie Dad? Well not exactly. He isn't exactly wearing psychedelic kaftans or shoulder-length hair. But his appearance is gradually softening as he adjusts to the new attitudes sweeping society.

1966 is supposed to be a best year ever because England is winning the World Cup, but Sunny Jim and the family don't even watch it. The Beatles are recording Sergeant Pepper and Swinging London has officially arrived.

Dad turns forty and his birthday coincides with Mum's hysterectomy operation. Both events mark the arrival of midlife, when outward success no longer protects us from the fear that life is passing us by. When Mum goes into hospital, Dad has work plus council meetings in the evenings. He arranges for Sunny Jim and the children to make daily visits to Mum, as he is unable to go.

By August 1966, an amateur family movie shows balls flying over cricket stumps, past seaweed and rocks, over the sea and up past chalk cliffs into the sky. There's just a tiny glimpse of Mum batting and the children fielding, proving Mum's on her feet again after the hysterectomy.

There's a new spirit of optimism in the world at large. With each year that passes, the American space mission brings mankind ever closer to the moon. Dramatic changes are happening across society: people find their voices in Civil Rights, Women's Liberation, anti-Vietnam demonstrations and three incredible days of Woodstock. With an upsurge of extraordinary new reforms, the loosening of laws on abortion and divorce combined with the Pill, adults are no longer trapped in bad marriages. Their lives can be freer, better and more equal.

Sunny Jim only gets a small fraction of the wider world events, filtered via his parents. When Dad comes home, he spouts the new management theories he is picking up at work. "Situational Leadership" means a parent needn't be consistent because he keeps adjusting his style as a child grows up. "Maslow's Hierarchy" means a parent ascends out of low-level concerns about food and shelter, towards the sunny uplands of love, achievement, self-awareness and creativity. "Theory Y" says a leader gets more from other people when he trusts them, rather than checking up all the time.

Sunny Jim notes, with scepticism, that these theories justify Dad's lax approach to parenting, and offer Dad greater freedom to do his own thing.

In spring 1967, Dad loses in the local council election, and after the initial shock, the blame lands on Jeremy Thorpe, a new and unpopular Liberal party leader with a scandalous personal life. Two weeks after Dad's defeat, Sunny Jim is climbing a slate-scree with Dad in the middle of Wales, and on their return to the farm where the family is camping, Auntie G and Uncle T are paying an unscheduled visit. Something is afoot. Mum's appointment at the Marriage Guidance Council happens shortly after the family returns home, and she goes alone.

With Dad's "Political Mission" blocked by the lost election, he has ants in his pants again. He invests his spare energy in the "Religious Mission" and begins working with the vicar on unity meetings, worship experiments with the Methodists and evening discussions with the Mormons. Dad encourages Sunny Jim's church Confirmation in October 1967. He is twelve years old. How could anyone foresee the events that would soon make Sunny Jim change his mind?

Dad's "Sociological Mission" brings "waifs and strays" into the home: Ibrahim, homeless while visiting from Egypt, Dorcas, young lonely paraplegic from church, Yvonne, a *'terribly nice'* unemployed teacher with a brain tumour and Paul, an ex-military officer with a depressed wife, a suicidal son and large appetite for drink. These few people arrive sometimes for meals, and occasionally stay the night, but it's a far cry from the larger ambition implied by Dad's "perfect mini-society".

More dramatic progress occurs in Dad's "Industrial Mission", when he resigns from the paper industry to become a polytechnic lecturer in London. Dad says this requires the family to move to Rochester, for a better train service to London. They find a bigger house to accommodate Mum's ageing aunt. Mum fiercely resists the move, but Dad wears her down as usual and, after the summer of 1968, the children change schools again.

Despite those upheavals and the loss of school friends, summer 1968 is one of the happiest for Sunny Jim, because of rewiring the Rochester house. There is no money for this unexpected expense, so Dad takes time off work to do the job himself. He chooses Sunny Jim to be his helper. Each morning, Sunny Jim sets off with Dad in the two-tone blue Vauxhall estate car (688 KO) from Maidstone to Rochester. They spend the day lifting floorboards, drilling holes in joists, mounting junction boxes, running wires beneath the floor and connecting sockets on the skirting boards. After three happy weeks the wiring is done, but August is over, and Dad disappears into the autumn.

Dad's appearance is changing. He has ditched the Brylcreem, and begins combing his hair forwards for a less shiny look. He grows a beard, then shaves it off, and then grows it again. Instead of the grey suit and shiny black shoes, he takes to a brown cardigan and suede Hush Puppies. He talks more often of his *'gilded cage'* and *'tearing up the rules'*. He plainly wants to be free.

As a lecturer in social sciences at North Western Poly based in London, Dad is suddenly everywhere else. His weeks are blanked out to "residential courses" at Hythe, Wilmslow, Banbury or Sawston. His days are fast and furious, packed with meetings up and down the country. He starts booking up the weekends for "personal growth meetings". His diary is full of deletions and insertions. He is losing interest in his missions with the church and the council, and there is less time for the family.

Dad begins secretly plotting with his new colleagues, the social science lecturers, to form a new consultancy called MKA. Clandestine meetings land them contracts with the polytechnic's top corporate clients: Ford, ICI and the Civil Service College.

Meanwhile, Sunny Jim is settling into a new school, struggling to adapt to a different syllabus and missing his old friends. One day that autumn, Sunny Jim runs into Dad in the hallway with a shiny silver transistor radio hanging around his neck that is filling the house with the noise of Radio 2. It's a bit of a surprise to see Dad and the new transistor radio is unexpected too. Sunny Jim just stares, silently blaming his absentee Dad for the move that uprooted everyone, for the disastrous school, for the loss of friends and for never being at home. Dad splutters apologetically: *'It was time to buy something for myself, after all these years of selflessly supporting other people'*.

Sunny Jim, moralistic after his Confirmation, feels only contempt for Dad's self-indulgence. According to Dad, the new house was expensive, and everyone had to economise, and now this: Dad is a hypocrite, saying one thing and doing something else, trashing the rules he himself imposed. Sunny Jim brushes by without a word, visualising in his mind's eye four uprooted children friendless at home, with their Mum looking out of the window, towards a husband who is sneaking away.

With the end of 1968 approaching, Mum has a serious car crash, with a jack-knifed lorry sliding sideways towards her down an icy hill. This slices open the roof of the Vauxhall Victor Estate (688 KO), bringing Mum within an inch or two of death. Fortunately she ducks, but is admitted to hospital for tests. Dad is too busy to visit, and by the weekend when he returns, Mum is discharged with "mild concussion". The car is a write-off, and Mum suffers splitting headaches. No one likes the turquoise Ford Cortina estate (GGK 845C) that replaces the Vauxhall.

After a strained first term in his new school, Sunny Jim begins to think of their house move in 1968 as Dad's first hammer blow. Two more are soon to follow.

*

The place of the family's next big drama was the Deben Estuary. In February 2016, Helen and I settled on a plan to visit. I hadn't been there since August 1969, almost forty-seven years earlier.

Clouds hung ominously. Helen didn't like the village of Bawdsey but she didn't say why. I didn't pay much attention because I was pulsing with anticipation, ready to relive a great adventure that happened there, the true significance of which I had never fully grasped.

A sign on a railing said in big black letters: *'No Swimming'*. A small white motorboat was dropping a passenger, under a sky that promised a serious drenching. The single word *'Ferry'* was nailed to the mast. The ferryman's face was weather-beaten red, and a black knitted hat was pulled down as far as the stud on his ear lobe. His body was a bundle packed warmly against the elements.

I began hesitantly: *'How much is it?'*
*'Three pounds like it says there on the sign'*. The ferryman didn't waste words.
We handed over the fare.
*'Sit over there'*.

I was anxious to continue: *'Does that include the return?'*
*'Like it says on the sign.'*
The sign was too small to read, but I was frustrated for a different reason: he'd shut down the conversation.

There were no other passengers. We faced the ferryman's back as he pointed the boat towards the far shore. The wind came from all angles and the Perspex screen hardly protected him. The tide was flowing in steadily from the sea, against a vigorous outflow from the river, just as it did when we swam here in August 1969.

I tried again: *'It looks like rain'*.
The ferryman looked gloomily at the heavy clouds: *'That's all I bloody need'*.

With the shore fast approaching, I braced myself to be more direct: *'May I ask you something?'* It felt clumsy.
Without looking round, the ferryman replied: *'You'd better get on with it'*.

With that tiny encouragement, I seized my chance: *'Does anyone ever swim this?'*

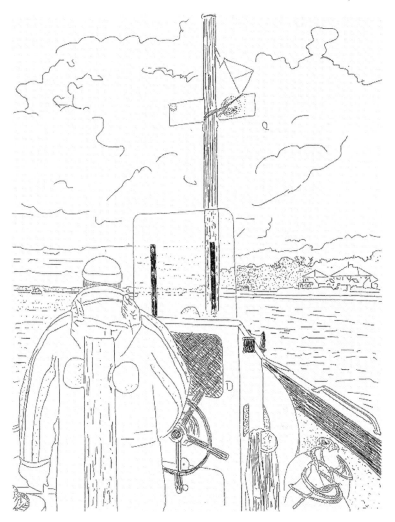

*'A few bloody fools each year, then we're running round trying to save them.'*

Emboldened, I continued: *'It's stupid to swim it then?'*
*'Two or three drown every year, on average.'*

After we landed on the Felixstowe side, Helen and I walked along the sea wall and around a Martello Tower. I was processing the fact that my great adventure was no such thing: it was blatantly foolish, not courageous at all. We browsed the fresh fish stalls, before heading back on the ferry.

During the second stage of our re-enactment, we followed Mum's twenty-five mile drive via Woodbridge when she went to meet the swimmers at the other side. We wound through those country lanes and I sensed Mum's misery. Helen asked: *'What was behind your Mum and Dad's argument?'*

I sided naturally with Dad for seeking adventure, while Mum wanted to keep things safe. Helen sided with Mum: *'Your Dad's beyond reckless. You nearly drowned. We Section people under the Mental Health Act for far less'.*

Then she began probing: *'Why was the fisherman who picked you up that day so angry?'*
My answer was confident: *'The survivor howls with pain. You can't live so close to water without losing family and friends to the tide'.*
At this, Helen's anger surfaced: *'And, your Dad endangered your lives'.* That was the plain truth.

I visualised Helen standing with Mum and my young brother, stern-faced on the far shore, while Dad and I and the others climbed out exhausted and shame-faced from the small rescue boat. Our adventure that I once regarded as a high point was the worst blow for Mum.

Helen hadn't finished: *'So why? Was your Dad trying to kill you?'*
That wasn't impossible. *'Surely you don't believe he was testing your faith?'*
Suddenly I felt certain: *'The God thing is a red herring'.* Finally, I'd admitted it: Dad was throwing in God towards something that mattered far more, but he wasn't willing to say what that was.

*'If not religion what is it?'*
I started thinking out loud: *'After the rescue, Dad's face said he had achieved something'.*

Then Helen was ready to give up: *'But after forty-seven years, why does it matter?'*
This made me defiant. It did matter because we were tantalisingly close to putting this to rest. With three of our

witnesses dead, and the other two unwilling to talk, it was down to us, and I was relying on Helen: *'Yes, it matters because of the silence'*.

And with that, the real answer burst out of me: *'This was an attack on our family by Dad. He was trying to break out, and that was too horrible to admit, hence the silence'*.

After this, it was useless to continue denying it. The move to Rochester a year earlier was an attack on the family that harmed everyone. The estuary swim was Dad's second hammer blow, just as confusing and far more dangerous. Dad was shaking the family off. He was making a break.

Yet unbelievably, after that terrible day at the estuary, life at home went on more or less as usual. We pretended everything was fine, although plainly it wasn't.

*

Helen and I returned from Bawdsey in February 2016, and I completed my reading of all the diaries. I summarised the most important bits, and mostly I did this alone. Helen's hip had hardly been troubling her since Bawdsey, and I sensed, with that urgency removed, her interest in the quest was waning.

Late one afternoon in March 2016, I climbed up into the attic to return the stack of old diaries to the black metal box. I saw the manila "Divorce" file that contained the boring solicitors' letters, and noted that even those deserved a look.

There in the attic, I skimmed through the file. The' letters relating to two divorces were filed in date order, but tucked behind them was a transparent plastic file, containing a sheet headed in Dad's upper case hand: *'REVELATION'*. Below this heading were the words: *'It happened on Trinity Sunday 1970…'*. This was the start of two foolscap pages filled with Dad's neat blue fountain pen writing. There was also a torn off half-page containing annotated triangles, bubbles and boxes, and a half page empty except for one word *'Comments?'* The papers had the musty smell of age, with folds suggesting they were once enveloped.

The night of the Revelation was unforgettable. In my mind I was using a capital R to give Dad the benefit of the doubt, but I had never really understood it. I turned to the diary entry for 24th May 1970:

*'Trinity Sunday 4am. Astonishing religious dream! Woke the family and told them, while we drank tea and swapped appalling jokes. 6am packed up camp. Left after breakfast'.*

Then I climbed downstairs from the attic, with the manila file containing the foolscap sheet, the 1970 diary, and a stack of letters. It was late afternoon and already dark outside. We sat in front of the fire to piece together the story of The Revelation. It turned out to be Dad's third hammer blow.

*

- **Settings:** May 1970 Dartmoor Campsite.
- **Props:** Interior of Bedford Dormobile.
- **Characters:** The family. Eve.

It is May half term, and the Saturday of Sunny Jim's fifteenth birthday. The family sets off in the Dormobile to go camping on Dartmoor. Sunny Jim is happy because it is his birthday, the Dormobile is new, a replacement for the hated Cortina, and this outing is a big treat. He still enjoys camping, despite his mixed feelings about the last camping trip when the estuary swim took place.

Inside the burgundy and cream Dormobile with its sliding front doors is a crowded mini-world, with sleeping space for four. That night Sunny Jim and his youngest brother are on bunks in the red and white striped elevating roof, above the parents' double bed, which is made out of all the seats pushed together. A canvas awning connects the Dormobile to a frame-tent where his sister and a brother are sleeping.

At 4 am, Dad begins spluttering and fizzing like a firework. He is talking rapidly, and waking everyone up. Dad looks crazy and it's scary. He sprawls on the double bed beaming strangely. He talks too fast to make sense. His body, bloated to fifteen stone by rich hotel food, makes excited jerky movements that shake the van.

Sunny Jim's sister comes in from the tent to find out what is
going on, leaving her brother asleep outside. Dad turns on the
light and beckons her to stay. She sits by the steering wheel.
Sunny Jim climbs down from his bunk and sits facing the kitchen
at the back. His eleven-year-old brother leans over from above.
Mum is lying along the edge of the double bed facing away.

Dad's eyes are darting madly around, until he slows down to
explain: *'I can't sleep, because of a marvellous dream in which
all of my questions were answered!'*
Mum doesn't move.

There is a crash as Sunny Jim's younger brother falls from the
overhead bunk onto his sister below. His sister screams and
sobs: *'Ayeee…. Agh… you broke my legs!'*
The young brother screams back: *'You broke my neck!'*
Their eyes meet and they start giggling. Sunny Jim joins in and
the giggles continue as a handy distraction, while Dad, still
beaming, looks bemused.

Mum turns round wearily, her eyes are red. The laughter stops.
Mum cuddles the brother, and strokes the sister's hair, then pulls
up her knees and sits between the sister and brother, as if in
solidarity. She looks blank like a zombie.

Dad starts shooting angry glances in all directions. He looks
confused. Sunny Jim wants to shrug and say: *'You're the one
making a scene Dad'*. But instead he picks up what Dad just
said: *'All of your questions are answered? Which questions do
you mean?'*

Dad is flustered: *'Questions, questions, questions…'*, then
continues in a firmer voice, *'about my belief, and God, and the
church, and HOW MUCH MORE'*, he emphasises those words,
*'this means more than just going to church on Sundays'*. It's
nonsense.

Condensation is streaming down the windows. It's dark outside.
Sunny Jim's Dad has turned manic. His mother is crumpled and
vacant. The family has fallen apart.

Sunny Jim and his sister are taking turns to head off a crisis. She steps in: *'Dad, we all go to church every Sunday. We're at school all week. There's no time left!'*

Dad returns to reason: *'This is not about going to church more often, but about HOW we do what we already do, in a much better, more Christian way'.* His eyes are shifting sideways, up and down, startled as if checking where he is. He looks at Mum. She looks back at a terrifying stranger, and bursts out sobbing.

Sunny Jim takes a turn: *'What is a "much better way"?'*
Dad's eyes check the others one by one, daughter, mother, and both sons, before replying: *'Mum and I work hard, to make the world a slightly happier place. We do this by being generous and helpful to people, not just selfish'.*

Sunny Jim's sister calmly offers a next question to Dad: *'So what difference does your dream make?'*
Dad replies: *'Everything is arranged in threes: Father, Son and Holy Spirit. The Holy Spirit is unlocking the godly part in me and it's my job to pass that on. For others it's God the Father or Jesus the Son who hold the key. When Mum and I help people in our work, we are unlocking the godly part in others…'.*

*

My throat was dry and my head throbbing as we put the story together in front of the fire that afternoon in March 2016, but my mind was numb. Even after all these years, I lacked any plausible explanation for what had happened to Dad that night. I caught myself sighing and sucking in air.

Helen was sceptical: *'Don't be taken in by your Dad!'*
But I was not taken in. I was just miserable, believing Dad might have lost his mind.
Helen smirked scornfully: *'Ha! Your Dad falls back on religion again. Pretending he's having a "revelation". Is there anything else?'*

There was more, but Helen was tired of it all, and I was far too confused to go into it. So tired and baffled, we took ourselves up to bed.

The next morning I awoke early, and sat down with cold determination to attack the manila folder, the 1970 diary and the pile of letters, seeking to extract a proper explanation of Dad's Revelation.

Leaping out from the 1970 diary entries were disturbing items that I had missed on first reading:

## Gave lift to Elizabeth.

- Midnight drive with Iris and Alexandria.
- Rang Felicity.
- Had meal with Iris in Taverna.
- Letter to Iris.
- Miserable.
- Depressed.
- Row at home.
- Met Trissie.
- Rang Eve.

Who were these women? Was Dad cheating on Mum? How could we explain the midnight drive, the meals, those moods and the row?

As we approached 12.30pm and lunch, I looked back over my morning's work and sighed: *'Oh God!'*
Helen said: *'Oh God what?'*
My mind was running in all sorts of different directions, but I had seven solid pieces of evidence to show.

I shuddered while handing over Item One. This was a letter to Dad dated 27th May 1970, the first of four letters from a woman called "Eve", in which she said: *'I'm mystified how you believe your talks with me last week helped towards your Revelation. I'm really not quite sure what I did, but I'm touched that you wanted to share such personal feelings with me, and that your wife encouraged you to do this'.*

Helen asked: *'But who is Eve?'*
*'She's a woman from work'.* There was a tremor in my voice, perhaps because Eve was just one of several women I had noticed in Dad's diary entries. Eve's tone of voice made the issue with Dad rather obvious: he was making advances.

I handed Helen Item Two, a letter from Mum to Dad also dated 27th May 1970: *'I am not surprised at your interest in Eve, and remembering your favourable comments on her red dress I'm not sure whether I should feel worried'.*

Helen asked: *'Why should your Mum write that? And what's the significance of the date?'*
Mum's letter and the letter from Eve were both written to Dad the day after my parents both visited Eve in her flat in Croydon. Helen frowned: *'And why was that?'*
*'Because Dad was trying to prove his marriage was solid, his interest in Eve was totally innocent and simply to do with God's work.'*

Helen saw straight through this: *'So he's a predator who's spotted Eve. He's using your Mum to vouch for his decency and get past Eve's defences'.*

The evidence against Dad was mounting, and my heart was sinking.

Item Three was a letter in green biro from Dad to Eve dated 9th June 1970, headed jokingly in capitals: *'NOT FOR PUBLICATION PLEASE BURN BEFORE READING!'* It conveyed Dad's feelings to Eve and his offer to help rebuild her life and career after a recent personal crisis. Dad had learned of Eve's circumstances in a "T-group" (more about T-groups later) they had both attended shortly before the Revelation, in which group members were required to disclose personal feelings and give tough feedback.

This letter to Eve began: *'You've said don't upset me with letters and phones I cannot fathom. And I'm saying you appeal to me in every way, simultaneously as a friend, a woman, a counsellor, an intelligence, a conscience, a cook, a colleague, a protégé – the lot because you are so open, healthy and trusting… '*

What followed was damning proof of Dad's position: *'I feel in no danger whatsoever of becoming the dreaded "in-love/total dependency" connection we both fear. All I ask is the ability to go on sharing with you a love and friendship we can both be proud of, which springs from the sincerest motives of helping one another without destroying anybody else's happiness. That's all, your move, D'.*

The fact that this letter was in Dad's box suggests it was returned by Eve.

In a further series of letters and calls to Eve, Dad invited her to a weekend visit to our house in Rochester for three-way meetings with Mum. Mum, in a letter to Dad, resisted this and proposed a *'cooling off period'* for Dad to clarify his true thoughts and feelings towards Eve, and for Eve, who was finding Dad's attentions upsetting, to recover equilibrium. Eve agreed to this and Dad went along with it too.

Throughout this period, Dad's repeated declarations of ultimate loyalty to Mum and to their marriage, implied just the opposite: I became certain of Dad's willingness to give up everything for Eve, including his family. He was sending Eve's letters to Mum, and Mum's letters to Eve, in exaggerated attempts to prove his honesty.

Helen said: *'That's part of the manipulation, and his ruse to seduce Eve'.*
I argued against the ruse theory: *'So what was the Revelation then?'*

Item Four was Dad's full handwritten account of the Revelation from the manila file that he dated 14th June 1970, three weeks after it actually occurred, perhaps written to clarify his own thoughts during the "cooling off period".

*'It happened on Trinity Sunday 1970 – three weeks ago on the edge of Dartmoor. Thoughts of religion were a long way from my mind. A stressful period of work had come to an end and at last I – we – had escaped for a week's family holiday. After a hard day's drive we were encamped.*

*'For years I have been an observer of Christian behaviour rather than a protagonist. My beliefs were never internalised. I was at odds with myself. And this had gone on for 43 years.*

*'Of late, a change in the nature of my work had increased the stresses in relation to my Christian upbringing. Was there really*

*a God, or were there just people? What did I really believe? This
was my state of mind when it happened.*

*'It was a blinding Revelation in the early hours of Trinity Sunday,
which answered all my questions and I am now for the first time
at peace with myself. The message will not satisfy everybody,
but it satisfies me, and it flies in the face of many traditions, and
yet makes room for them all.*

*'God is a Trinity, three persons in one, as a triangle: Father,
Son. Holy Spirit. There is perfect intercommunication between
the three elements. Some people communicate with the Father,
accepting the authority of the church, with a strong sense
of "sinning" when its code of rules is transgressed. Others
communicate more readily with Jesus Christ, they have a friend
in Jesus. For me this never worked. I found it easier to address
my prayers to the father, seeking his approval of, or forgiveness
for my actions.*

*'The other class of Christians lets the Holy Spirit govern their
lives. They have no need to go to church, or to say their prayers
regularly or for any explicit religious observance.*

*'Then there is a fourth class, the agnostics or humanists, who do
not accept God at all, and will often belittle or oppose him.*

*'Of these four attitudes to God, I now know the right one for
me is the third, ie. the Holy Spirit. Moreover, the whole of life
is now a conscious effort to provide the same high degree of
communication between people as exists within God. Life is the
conscious spawning of further triangles, modelled on the Trinity.*

*'Thus, the bringing of a new person into the Christian fellowship
is to build communication outwards from myself, and from the
Holy Spirit, until trust and reciprocal communication is returned.*

*'Likewise, in the making of new friendship I extend trust and
communication towards my new friend, but I endeavour to link
them with any existing friends, such that neither friendship is in
any way threatened by the other.*

*'Every completed triangle becomes strong enough to begin*

*"spawning" other triangles, and a rapidly growing movement can become contagious. Most attempts at solving the world's problems, produce opposition, frustration and failure, because they start at a "macro" scale, in terms of numbers rather than unique human beings. By starting within oneself (ie. on a "micro" scale) and building outwards, we can start a growing movement of honest relationships, based on individuals rather than in the mass.*

*'To sum up, if anybody were to ask me 'What or who is God?' I would need to write a list which would be:*

*'GOD is a trinity of inter-dependency*
*part of us all*
*trust, love, honesty of relationships*
*free communication*
*giving before receiving*
*accepting what you cannot see*
*freedom to judge for yourself*
*friendship without threat*
*creating higher goals in conflict situations so that both sides can win*
*... and lots more.*

*'There just isn't any divergence between Christianity and Humanism any longer, and that is why I am now at peace. I hope that what I have written can help others to share this feeling.'*

I read this again and again that morning, and heard Dad's voice persuasive, logical and sincere.  But who was he trying to convince? I showed Helen his diagram of triangles, bubbles and boxes, and the sheet he attached for Mum's comments, which Mum left blank. I can imagine Mum's worried frown.

When Helen put down Dad's Revelation paper, she laughed:
*'Don't you dare propose an eternal triangle!'*
I replied with dire seriousness: *'Dad wrote this in total sincerity'.*

After that urge to speak up for Dad, I handed over Item Five, the carbon copy of Dad's poem to Eve on 22nd June 1970, just eight days after his "sincere" account of the Revelation:

*'In London's fair city one week late in May*
*A friendship I found which will last many a day*
*With a maiden whose wavelength and mine duplicate*
*An experience worthy to exhilarate*

*'Trinity Sunday a truth was revealed*
*And my internal stresses were suddenly healed*
*On Dartmoor to the family I told in full spate*
*The factors behind my excitable state*

*'Part of the value you have Eve for me*
*Is the frankness with which we can speak fancy-free*
*So if after cooling off you're still my close friend*
*Won't you please come and visit our house next weekend?'*

Unable to contain his excitable feelings, Dad sent this poem to Eve in the midst of the "cooling off period" they had all agreed upon.
Helen said: *'So suddenly it's all about Eve again and nothing to do with religion'.*

But it wasn't one or the other, it was both at the same time. Dad was just as excited about Eve as about the Revelation, and in his mind the two were connected. He was making himself a protagonist, trusting that the Holy Spirit was propelling him in his service to God. The poem that appears an expression of reckless abandon was in Dad's fevered mind the enacting of a religious imperative. It happened also to follow his lust, and to provide a handy defence against forthcoming charges at work regarding Dad's improper behaviour towards Eve.

Item Six was a letter from Eve to Dad dated 25th June 1970 in which she said: *'Many thanks for your letter/poem. I have to tell you that I've been re-instated in my liaison officer role'.*

Helen asked: *'What's that about her role?'*
I explained: *'Eve had been suspended at work because of Dad'.*

Dad and Eve were counterparts. She worked for ICI managing the account with Dad's firm MKA, where Dad was the one who managed the account with ICI. Their colleagues on both sides could see that Dad was smitten. ICI suspended Eve and placed

MKA's contract under review. But after an investigation cleared Eve's name, Dad was, in his own words, *'given his marching orders'.*

I handed over Item Seven, a letter from Eve to Dad dated 1st July 1970: *'The tone of your letters leads me to believe you haven't listened to my repeated pleas. I fear I'm going to have to hurt you and this is the last thing I want to do'.* It was solemn, concerned for Dad and apologetic.

Helen asked: *'Was he stalking her?'*
I swallowed and nodded: *'Yes, and now Eve is dumping him. But the intensity of Dad's phone calls, letters and postcards suggests he won't easily be dumped'.*

Helen tried out a possible conclusion: *'Your Dad's smitten by Eve, this compromises them both at work, endangering their jobs and jeopardising the contract with ICI. Dad's messed up big time, and the Revelation is his lie to himself to escape responsibility'.*

This almost nailed it, but if Helen had spent that May 1970 night in the Dormobile with us, Dad's manic eyes would have convinced her of Dad's sincerity. How could he fake those? In Dad's defence, I pointed out how many people he had told about the Revelation: Eve, Mum, his children and various colleagues at work. He stored the handwritten account, along with all these letters and the poem in the black secret box until he died in 2000, when it was handed over to me. Religion was his thing. He had brought up his four children in the church and recorded in his diaries their dates of Confirmation. Two of these confirmations were in 1970, book-ending the Revelation in May.

Helen argued back: *'This only proves he was confused about religion and lying to himself about Eve'.*

With her mouth pulled down in disgust she brought this to a close: *'As for the Dormobile, it's a Sexmobile more like. And the rest, surprise, surprise, is that well-known story about sex trumping religion!'*

*

After our discussion ended, I wanted to be theatre director again, at a safe enough distance to look objectively on all this evidence. The imagined triangles in Dad's "revelation" let him fit everything neatly together, but his lustful feelings towards Eve didn't fit easily into a marriage. His dream of a triangle with Mum and Eve as the work of the Holy Spirit let him off the hook, but neither Eve nor Mum was buying it. Eve said it was unfathomable, but Mum guessed it was a mask to cover up Dad's inconvenient feelings, his wish to seduce Eve and the need to save his job. Mum's silence on this was for the sake of their marriage, and because of this, Dad's hypocrisy wasn't exposed.

So far so good, but I was concerned for Sunny Jim. I felt for him in the shocking experience of Dad's Revelation at 4 am in the Dormobile. Three years earlier at his Confirmation at the tender age of twelve, Dad had encouraged Sunny Jim to commit his adult life to the church. For a year or so Sunny Jim carried a cross at the front of the procession in church, and served white wafers and a silver goblet of wine beside the curate during Communion. When Dad's "revelation" arrived, this cast doubt on Dad's religion and Dad's credibility. That doubt turned into scepticism. Either the balance of Dad's mind was disturbed, or Dad's "revelation" was a big fat lie.

At lunch that day, Helen and I were puzzling at the mayhem Dad created in our family. After the unwanted house move in 1968, the estuary swim in 1969, the "revelation" was Dad's third hammer blow to the marriage while he was in the grip of many demons: religion, unfulfilled ambitions towards politics, industry, society, human potential... and his attraction towards other women. Dad's behaviour was cruel to his wife and family, and sufficient grounds for divorce. If divorce was what Dad wanted, what better rationale for Dad's unkind behaviour, but Dad wasn't being rational.

By this point in the story I had lost objectivity. I was ready to give Sunny Jim a big thank-you hug, and to resign from my role as theatre director. In an attempt to recover perspective, I ran through what happened next: Dad was removed by his boss from the ICI contract, and ordered to sever links with Eve. His job was on the line, but he kept all this secret and, to the best of my knowledge, he never spoke again about the "revelation" and these related events. I suspect he preferred to believe he was chosen by God to receive that dream, and we can call that a Messiah Delusion.

As Helen and I finished our lunch, my feeling was despair: *'Dad's lost in Lala land. Lying to his family and leaving everyone totally in the dark!'*

I was becoming certain Mum was right: it looked a lot like twenty wasted years, and my parent's story was looking tragic. Despite Mum's best efforts to embark on a new life, she was turning into her mother who also lost her husband. Meanwhile Dad, pulled away from his family by his "selfless" work, was turning into his father.

Neither of my parents had totally given up on their marriage, and both were soon to play a part in trying to put things right.

# Part Four:
## Regarding Human Potential

## Chapter 16: Growth of The Movement

In April 2016, I attended an exhibition at the Sackler Serpentine Gallery in Hyde Park, determined to see things from Dad's perspective.

London's rush hour crush was easing as the tube brought me to Lancaster Gate. I walked south, beside grassy lawns and the distant swollen shapes of corporate buildings, which cut into a dull grey sky. Through the trees, I glimpsed the Sackler's white prawn cracker roof.

A bearded hipster in black, standing in the entrance, guessed my destination: *'The exhibition on Organising?'*

When I nodded he rotated his arm lazily: *'It's all around, left for yesterday's idealism, and right for where this has landed us. Enjoy!'*

A wall-mounted slogan *'Utopia or oblivion?'* carried me back in time and summed up the idealism of the Sixties: something impossibly wonderful to commit to, and why not? The displays were low key against a bare brick interior, and the empty-looking gallery was an ideal space to reflect.

At the start of 1970 Dad and his colleagues at the polytechnic opened the doors to a new consultancy called Marshall Krakow Associates (MKA). This turned into what I called the "Dormobile Year" in which Dad was propelled by inexplicable forces related to the many females whose names appeared in the diary, and more specifically to Eve and the "revelation".

During this year, Dad let it be known that he was part of a "Human Potential Movement". His sister later told me about *'those dreadful American self-awareness courses'* that drew Dad into a culture of *'selfish-gratification'*. The family was not impressed, but Dad waved off all criticism.

While remembering this, I was climbing aluminium steps at the exhibition, the wall beside me describing the USA's "behavioural science technology" coming out of their National Training Laboratory (NTL), which caught the interest of those business leaders in the Sixties. Top leaders in the western world, commanding vast bureaucracies, were horrified at a meltdown sweeping society. They saw anti-war riots, civil rights, leftists, communists and hippies. An anti-authoritarian counter-culture threatened to destroy their corporations and topple those in charge. Survival depended on these leaders making radical shifts in their leadership styles.

The National Training Laboratory (NTL) in Bethel, Maine, funded by the US Navy, had enrolled psychologists to produce a "Group Dynamics" methodology aimed at preventing another war, by dissolving the authority of war-mongering dictators, be they fascists or communists. At the same time a "Human Potential Movement" being born in California was inspiring its followers with a scale of ambition so staggering it beggared belief, and Dad bought into it. The Movement sought to bring the globe into a new post-war era, promising peace and fulfilment to all, unprecedented in the history of humanity. It would be like a big bright future combining Christmas, heaven and peace on earth. Dad saw his "industrial mission" and the spawning of "perfect Mini-Societies" as a practical step towards this dream.

When NTL began to recruit partner organisations to spread its Group Dynamics Training into big corporations, Dad's new employer, MKA, took up a license. After that MKA didn't look back.

As I mounted the last aluminium step, I saw laid out across a scaffolding platform models of the latest corporate buildings, flat and round in style, and quite unlike the modernist, monolithic towers of the Sixties. These were being built today for Apple, GCHQ and several others, with some common features: open plan offices surrounding a central atrium, with recreation areas to encourage 'creativity' and 'free-flowing communication' in their 'empowered' workers. Such workplaces were the future according to that exhibition in April 2016, and it made me wonder if Dad and his colleagues at MKA were prescient.

Dad taught me that you can't order someone to be creative; instead there's a magic you have to unleash. He said the word "com-pany" means eating bread together, and whether it's a factory, a shop or a hospital, an underlying spirit of creativity and cooperation is hidden there, inside everyone, just waiting to be unlocked. He imagined work in the future would be based on trusting people and nurturing their creativity, rather than simply giving and receiving orders. Companies operating in the new way would expand and offer the jobs to put food on the tables at home, while companies sticking to the old ways would die. It was simply Darwin's survival of the fittest.

Social scientists, like Dad stated to work with top business leaders towards creating these liberated workplaces. Dad and the MKA faculty ran a week-long programme with around twenty senior managers. It started on Monday with two MKA trainers in a classroom delivering dry lectures on "theories of leadership" and "stages in human development" to those senior managers sitting at desks. Inevitably their pupils became bored and before Monday lunchtime they rebelled against the trainers' domineering style. On the Monday afternoon, the trainers challenged the leaders to take back control and organise themselves into teams to identify and tackle their real business problems. The week became a succession of crises followed by post-mortems in which unusually open feedback was employed to expose the faults in an ingrained and authoritarian leadership style. The aim was to accelerate a company's transformation towards creative and flexible teamwork. By the end of the week, each group of attendees was eager to attend more programmes and spread the new approach.

It was in MKA's interest to stoke this demand. They imported all available methods from the US including "T-groups" (also called Sensitivity Training) and "N-Groups" (also called Encounter Groups). The new "Human Potential Movement" (HPM) springing to life in California was spreading its doctrine and methods globally through the branches of an "Association for Humanistic Psychology" (AHP). The partners in MKA played a part in setting up a new AHP branch in London.

On the rare occasions when Dad's colleagues visited our home, their loud confident manner made them appear drunk on success. Dad was caught up in the hubris at MKA and building his own links to the Human Potential Movement, which he hoped could give birth to his dreamed of "mini-society". He didn't mind that he was drifting away from his family and from all that he had ever held dear. After his "revelation", Dad had little need to worry about right or wrong. He was trusting himself and the Human Potential Movement was becoming his religion.

I descended the aluminium steps, and visited the remaining displays, to find that the "hackers" we often dismiss as anarchists or mavericks are in fact the new creatives. These talented individuals have developed the secure, Open Source systems upon which many of today's stock-markets and top corporations rely. Companies like Apple and GCHQ need ways to attract such talent and to build workplace cultures in which their people will communicate as freely and openly as the hackers do.

Surprisingly, the anti-authoritarian work environments that were encouraged in the Sixties by the Human Potential Movement, are at last being manifest in many of our most successful organisations.

# Chapter 17: Secrets and Lies

It was May 2016 and one year since the brief bliss of "Peak Bubble" in Majorca. I looked through the crack in the bedroom curtains and, instead of Mediterranean sunshine, dark clouds signalled a storm approaching. After twelve months of struggle to break a silence and overcome a taboo, the exhibition at the Sackler had produced a few tiny reasons to forgive a father who was clearly neglectful, obsessed and driven by demons. He was also building a better world, or trying to, but he was naive, and there were more troubles ahead.

These mixed feelings told me I needed a break. Later that morning when the sky cleared, I went for a long cycle ride along the river. Fresh air on my skin, bright green leaves, and white candles on the horse chestnut trees lifted my spirits and helped me forget myself.

Helen's jibe over dinner that evening brought us back to the story: *'When it comes to your Dad, I'm torn between prison and mental hospital, but veering towards hanging him up by the toenails!'*

During 1970, Dad's physical and mental condition was fast deteriorating. After the events surrounding the "revelation" put him in a serious pickle, there were odd hints that Mum and Dad were trying to change, in the form of surprising secrets about their lives, disclosed in clumsy attempts at openness from which I shrank.

As theatre director I re-enacted the headline events on the dining table stage, using the index cards and all the usual sources. As usual, the details flooded back.

*

- **Settings:** Summer 1970, MKA office
- **Props:** Letters. Postcards. Phone box.
- **Characters:** Eve, Dad, two MKA partners

It is unclear whether Dad will just be sacked from the ICI client account or, more seriously, from MKA his employer, with the consequent loss of salary and the wherewithal to pay our mortgage at home.

Dad's disciplinary meeting with the two MKA partners is unusually frank because of their loyalties to the Human Potential Movement. The first partner, Brian Marshall, is on the founding committee of Britain's new Association for Humanistic Psychology (AHP). The other partner, Pieter Krakow, is on the point of finishing his PhD with the University of Rotterdam into the subject of "Human Growth and Potential". Those two partners are idealists made wealthy by deploying their large team of social scientists to run executive training programmes in Ford, ICI, Reed Paper Group, the Civil Service and other top organisations.

None of those three doubts that MKA's initial success will continue, despite Dad's recent difficulties. Dad opens the disciplinary meeting facing those two partners who are stern-faced, and makes an immediate proposal to give "feedback" about the recent difficulties, and this begins his fightback. To those in the Human Potential Movement "feedback" is a hallowed gift, and the refusal to take receive it would be heresy: so the partners accept. Dad goes on to describe his removal from the ICI account as *'autocratic'* and *'against the values of MKA'*, and the partners don't demur. Dad admits to being *'out of his depth'* due to *'inexperience'* and *'lack of necessary training'*. The partners ask him for specific examples, which Dad supplies. After a few minutes, the debacle with ICI has been recast as a *'terrible misunderstanding'*. The partners agree to give Dad another chance, and Pieter Krakow offers Dad *'mentoring'*, which Dad is pleased to accept.

As a result, Dad is kept on by MKA, and all three, through the process of feedback, have reconfirmed their faith in the Human Potential Movement.

*

When I played this scene back to Helen, she was sarcastic: *'So he's holding onto his job, but is he also holding onto his sanity and his family? Ooops, no, he's already lost his sanity!'*

We laughed with relief, and perhaps this buoyed us up ready for the trickier scenes to follow, towards which I sought Helen's help.

*

- **Settings:** Summer 1970, Dormobile
- **Props:** Carl Rogers' book
- **Characters:** Dad, Sunny Jim

After the "revelation" in May 1970, Sunny Jim is becoming a long-haired, disillusioned teenager. His morning paper round brings money to fund his greater independence. He has stopped going to church. He wants to be like his friends at school. He thinks Dad is off his rocker.

This is when Dad starts telling Sunny Jim secrets Sunny Jim does not want to know. He is a passenger with Dad, driving to Hastings to visit Grandma whose health is declining. Dad is saying *'Pieter this and Pieter that'*, as if Pieter Krakow, the partner at work, is some kind of god. Dad says Pieter recently gave him an interesting question: *'Why do you do so much for others? It's always for your family, for God, or the good of the firm, and why is it never for you?'*

*

Helen and I were testing out this scene. I spoke out those words from Pieter and they hit the nail on the head because Helen burst out: *'No one ever pretended to be as squeaky clean as your dad!'*

After this interruption, we returned to the scene.

*

Sunny Jim is in the car with Dad who is enthralled about his recent conversation with Pieter, in which he decided to become a little more selfish, and a little bit more open, because until he *'showed his cards'*, no one would trust him.

Sunny Jim doesn't agree that Dad is doing much for others, because lately Dad is mostly pleasing himself. Sunny Jim assumes Dad wants to prove to his son that Pieter holds him in high esteem. And perhaps, in a roundabout way, Dad is trying out Pieter's advice: to be a bit more open.

But then Dad moves into embarrassing territory. He says he disclosed to Pieter the *'personal problem'* that got him into difficulty at ICI. It was about *'the limits of marriage'*, his *'need for freedom'* to build new relationships, after a *'cooling of passions at home'*. Dad is spilling out such lurid detail that Sunny Jim's mind is racing.

*

Helen burst out: *'Well, surprise, surprise! A man uproots his family, almost succeeds in drowning them, and pretends to become the Holy Spirit to cover up his lust for a woman at work. Why wouldn't his wife lose interest?'*

We returned to Sunny Jim's car journey.

*

Dad is telling Sunny Jim about the book Pieter lent him, in which the famous psychologist called Carl Rogers advises us to express ourselves *'openly and freely'* through the body.

*

Helen couldn't resist the joke: *'Wasn't he hoping to do that with Eve?'*
She was right: I accepted that Dad lusted after Eve.

We returned to the scene.

*

Dad is telling Sunny Jim that Mum refuses the advice of Carl Rogers, by being *'closed'* and *'unwilling to grow'*. Sunny Jim refuses to listen to Dad finding fault with Mum. It's dangerous ground that reminds Sunny Jim of his parents' argument at the estuary. Sunny Jim keeps quiet while Dad continues: Pieter didn't stop at lending Dad the book, he also recommended a famous

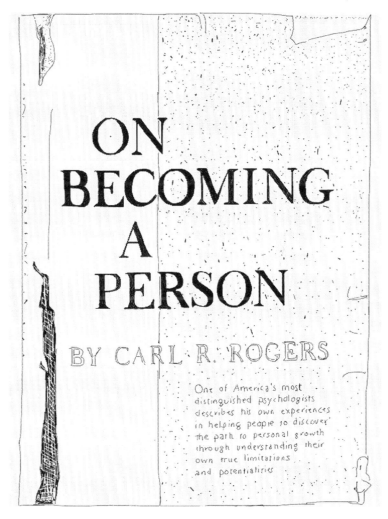

ON
BECOMING
A
PERSON

BY CARL R. ROGERS

One of America's most
distinguished psychologists
describes his own experiences
in helping people to discover
the path to personal growth
through understanding their
own true limitations
and potentialities

Gestalt therapist to *'remove the blocks to expressing himself freely'*. The therapist, Doktor Spiel, was visiting from America in the autumn and Dad was looking forward to the session.

*

That was Dad's secret.

Helen remarked: *'Dead dodgy or what? And what help do you need from me?'*

I said: *'Wait a minute. First I'll tell you Mum's secret.'*

The secret Mum told Sunny Jim in autumn 1970 was related to the secret Dad told Sunny Jim in the car that summer on the way to Hastings.

\*

Mum stops Sunny Jim on the stairs and begins a strange interrogation: *'I need to ask you something'*.
Sunny Jim says: *'OK'*.
Mum continues: *'What do you know about the physical side of a marriage?'*

Sunny Jim clams up: *'Nothing much, since I have no experience'*. He can't fathom what Mum's after.

Mum presses on: *'Do you know how alcohol affects things?'*
Sunny Jim replies: *'I assume it's not helpful'*.
Mum nods: *'That's right. It isn't helpful'*.

This leaves Sunny Jim perplexed. He takes a stab at the answer: *'Are you talking about Brewer's Droop?'*
Mum nods.

\*

Helen interrupted: *'Why was your Mum bringing this up?'*
I replied: *'Because she's telling Sunny Jim something about Dad'*.
We returned to the story.

\*

Mum puts on an agonised face and tells Sunny Jim that Dad is questioning everything, complaining he got married too young and he wants the freedom to go after other women.

Mum's eyes are watery and she presses on to tell Sunny Jim it is perfectly normal to have some *'unevenness'* in a marriage with this occasional *'loss of spark'*.

Sunny Jim is nodding because he wants to get it over with.

He doesn't enjoy thinking about what happens in his parents' bedroom.
But Mum hasn't finished: *'Dad is having a midlife crisis'.*

This sounds terrible, but it helps Sunny Jim appreciate Dad's position.

*

Helen cut in again: *'Did she say anything more?'*
I replied: *'OK, listen up for something juicy'.*

*

Mum tells Sunny Jim that a charlatan doctor has diagnosed Dad as *'sexually repressed'. She uses those exact words.*

Mum says this doctor brought Dad up onto a stage at a public meeting, and blurted out about his "loss of spark" in front of a hundred strangers. As a medical practice, she says this is unethical and possibly dangerous, but on Dad's part it shows *'exceptionally poor judgement'*, and consequently Dad is *'suffering side effects'.*

Sunny Jim brings this to a close: *'Can we do anything about it?'*
Mum says: *'No, I just wanted you to know, that's all'.*

*

That was Mum's secret.

Helen asked: *'Was this quack the one your dad mentioned, Doktor Spiel?'*
I nodded.

*'Is this part you want help with?'*
I nodded and smiled.

Helen smiled back, but looked wary: *'OK, let's give it a go'.*

It was after dinner, around seven in the evening and we were sitting at the dining table with glasses of wine. I put on Buena

Vista Social Club to lighten our mood and inspire us for the task ahead. Samba rhythms from Cuba were wafting past our ears and, with the iPad propped open, we watched five short YouTube clips from the late 1960s featuring Doktor Frederic Spiel working as a therapist live on the stage with his clients in a hall. Spiel was a character.

I opened a fresh page in my notebook and wrote a first sentence:

*A world-renowned new age guru from California is on the stage for a performance that he calls his "circus".*
*Tickets are scarce and Dad is one of the lucky ones.*
*Smoke from the guru's cigarette mingles with the fluffy grey hair that sprouts uncontrollably from the sides of his head. His straggly beard blurs the edges of his face.*

I passed the notebook to Helen, who sucked on her pen, before she began scribbling:

*We are viewing this through a camera that takes in the whole scene. Three chairs nestle round the low table before an audience of about a hundred, seated in rows. A microphone on a chrome stand points at the hairy guru on the left, and another microphone at two empty chairs on the right.*
*Speaking English with a strong German accent, the guru's voice is tired, but his eyes are lively, darting here and there. His "show" begins with a short explanation:*

Helen passed me the notebook and I continued:

*Spiel: 'We work in the here and now, not deep, but on the surface, with the obvious. The technique is not to explain things, but to provide the person with opportunities to understand. I concentrate on the non-verbal, as this is less liable to self-deception. Now, who has a problem to bring us?'*
*A man with short black hair, a beard and a crumpled suit springs to his feet: 'I do'.*
*Spiel: 'What is the problem you want to bring?'*

Helen took the notebook, paused, then scribbled happily while she moved to the rhythm, until she returned the notebook with a slight giggle. I read her second contribution:

*Man: 'Flaccidity'.*
*Sniggers across the audience, then a hush as Spiel, undeterred,*
*starts to focus: 'And specifically what?'*
*Man: 'You could say failure to rise to the occasion'.*
*There are gasps and hoots.*

I adopted the stance of the therapist:

*Spiel challenges everyone: 'Why do you all laugh? And sir, why*
*'you could say'? Is this a real problem of sexual performance, or*
*are you just joking?'*
*Man: 'I am serious and it is real'.*
*Spiel: 'Then come up and sit here on the chair next to me'.*
*The man comes onto the stage and Spiel begins the therapy: 'Tell*
*me what you are experiencing, here and now'.*

I returned the notebook, and it was Helen's turn:

*Man: 'My forehead is hot, and I can't talk to you here'.*
*Spiel: 'Speak to me in that chair to the left of you'.*
*The man turns to address the empty chair on his left: 'Can I talk*
*to you here?'*
*Spiel (without moving) replies: 'Yes'.*

*The man continues: 'I am not afraid to talk to you, but others*
*are watching me'. He nods at the camera, '...and over here', he*
*nods at the audience.*
*Spiel: 'Now address the camera. What will you say to the*
*camera?'*
*The man says: 'I have clammed up'.*

I knew from the YouTube videos exactly where to go next:

*Spiel: 'Now, sir, go into the empty chair, and be the camera*
*looking back at the flaccid man. If the camera had words to say*
*to him ...'*
*Man as camera: 'Now I am speaking to the flaccid man... You*
*are bringing something real, and you want to be taken seriously'.*
*Spiel: 'Now come back into the first chair, be yourself and go on'.*
*The man moves back and continues: 'I am at ease. I can talk to*
*you now'.*

*Spiel: 'What are you noticing?'*
*Man: 'Words are coming to me'.*

Then Helen became the therapist:

*Spiel: 'I want you to move into the empty chair and pretend to unzip your flies, then to speak back to yourself from that part of you'.*
*The man moves into the empty chair and speaks as if from his trousers: 'I can surprise you, and I can disappoint you. I can be here when I am not needed, and not here when I am needed...'*

The blood rose to my face: *'My God Helen!'*
She giggled and I picked up the pen:

*Spiel: 'Now come back into the first chair and continue this dialogue with your trousers, but from your side'.*
*The man returns to his chair and continues: 'When you don't show up I am horribly disappointed...'*
*Spiel interjects: 'And what are you aware of right now sir?'*

*Man: 'I am surprising myself, I'm totally present, despite everything and everyone watching, I am being open and honest'.*
*Spiel: 'Now move again into the second chair, and speak back to yourself from your trousers'.*

Helen dashed off the next part:

*The man moves and speaks from his trousers: 'When you are like this, fully present, then I am ready, and fully present too'.*
*Spiel: 'Now move back into the first chair...'*
*The man moves.*
*Spiel: 'And how are you now?'*
*The man smiling and relaxed: 'Good. Feeling much... better'.*

*Spiel addresses the audience:*

Helen handed me the notebook to bring the session to a close:

*Spiel: 'We see again and again, the inner war of conflict in a patient weakens him, while every bit of integration brings him*

*strength. This man is in conflict, sexually repressed and by
acting out the ailing parts of himself, he frees up and awakens
from the nightmare of his existence. Sir, you may go'.
The man shocked to be so brutally summed up, leaves the stage
and instead of returning to his place in the audience, picks up his
briefcase and departs.*

Helen shook her head in despair *'How mad is that?'* she said. We
both laughed.

*

The following morning, Helen re-read our session with Doktor
Spiel: *'Why were we sitting here last night writing this?'*

I was quite clear: *'Because Mum and Dad both spilled the secret
about Dad's visit to Doktor Spiel, and Dad kept reporting "sex
failures" in his diary'.*

*'And why did your parents tell you their personal secrets?'*
I said Mum was preparing me in case Dad walked away. And Dad
had a different reason: he just needed to get it off his chest, to
benefit himself, not to benefit me.

Then I asked my question: *'Was it fun re-enacting the Spiel
session?'* I wanted Helen to agree, and I answered my own
question: *'Yes'.*
She objected: *'But we can't prove this was how Dad's session
went 46 years ago'.*
I agreed: *'No, but we do know that's how Spiel worked, that Dad
was diagnosed sexually repressed, and he chose therapy on the
public stage instead of a more sensible private consultation. I'm
guessing that was Pieter's advice'.*

We made a cup of coffee and sat at the dining table to complete
a short final scene in 1970 around our dining table in Rochester.

On 16th December 1970, my sister, just seventeen, had her first
and last driving lesson conducted by Dad.

*

- **Setting:** December 1970. White Fiat 500. Dining Room Rochester.
- **Props:** Macaroni cheese, dining table
- **Characters:** Mum, Dad, The Boys, Sister.

Sunny Jim is fifteen years old, sitting at a laid table with his brothers, and waiting for supper to arrive. Their sister is nowhere to be seen. Dad is also at the table.

Mum enters from the kitchen, down the step, past the tropical fish tank, and drops a hot dish of scorched macaroni cheese onto the table.
She addresses Dad breezily: *'How was the lesson, darling?'*
*'Shaky at first, but improving',* Dad says smiling. *'She's getting the hang of it!'*

Mum and Dad are being pleasant, to set an example to The Boys. Sunny Jim is trying to figure out what is really going on.

Like ping pong, The Boys are tracking the ball that bounces between the parents, their heads moving from one side to the other. Mum sits down: *'Really? I'm so pleased!'* She says this distractedly as if to trick her opponent, before suddenly she pounces: *'And how did the dent arrive?'*

Dad puts on a look of alarm: *'Dent?'*
Mum continues: *'I'm sure it was nothing much',* then a second later, when Dad least expects it, Mum plays the ball back firmly: *'But it's on the front wing of **my** little Fiat'.*

Dad is trapped, and tries to shorten his moment of humiliation: *'Can we please **not** dwell on the details?'*
Mum appears to soften: *'You can at least tell me, what DID happen?'* but her hackles are rising.

Sensing this, The Boys' eyes move expectantly back to Dad. *'It really wasn't her fault.'* Dad is defending his daughter, while still withholding the story.

Mum slams the ball back: *'I'm sure it wasn't… but WHAT wasn't?'*

Dad sighs and gives in: *'We were driving under the motorway, and passing a horse-rider, when the horse swerved into our path. No one was hurt. She... brought the car to a halt, but...'.*

The story is comical. The sister's first driving lesson has not gone well. Sunny Jim tests his understanding: *'She drove her car into a horse?'*
Mum ignores this and continues the tussle with Dad: *'BUT what?'*
Dad hesitates: *'She found it over-whelming, so we swapped, and continued the lesson'.*

Dad's *'overwhelming'* makes the story juicier, and everyone is forgetting the food.

Sunny Jim's middle brother repeats his line: *'She drove her car into a horse?'*
Mum ignores this too, because she is pursuing Dad: *'And how is her confidence now?'*
Dad drops his head, stares at the table, then puts on a brave face: *'Since we got home she has stopped crying, and is much calmer'.*

Mum looks alarmed: *'Is she really OK? Why isn't she here at the table?'*
Dad makes an excuse: *'I wanted her to go back behind the wheel but she kept refusing'.*

At the perfect moment the sister enters the room, eyes down, silent. With a forced smile, Dad seizes the chance to recover: *'Ah here she is!'*

Finally the youngest brother catches on, and banging the table begins to chant: *'She drove her car into a horse! She drove her car into a horse!'*
The Boys all join in: *'She drove her car into a horse...'*

Dad flushes and shouts: *'Stop it boys!'*
Reluctantly The Boys let their chant die, and drop their eyes to the floor.

The sister flushes and dashes out.
Dad says to Mum: *'I think she'll be OK for our next lesson...'* But

Mum is dashing out to comfort her daughter.

The youngest boy whispers: *'Pants on fire!'* and The Boys break into giggles, but Dad doesn't respond because he doesn't understand. The Boys have caught Dad covering up the truth. Dad's not completely there. He has lost his place.

*

In May 2016, as theatre director watching what that once happy family had become, I felt sadness. The driving lesson was a disaster, but worse, it exposed Dad's instinct to hide from unpleasant truths, and highlighted Mum's capacity to root him out.

The youngest brother's *'pants on fire'* pointed to Dad's dishonesty, denial and self-defence. With this, Dad confirmed The Boys' suspicions about Dad. After being kept so many years in the dark, the lights were finally on and The Boys' happiness was expressed in their chanting and giggling.

Given the mounting evidence that Dad wanted to escape, what happened next was unexpected.

*

Two weeks later, it is Christmas 1970 and Dad excels himself. His face is aglow as he makes the happy announcement: *'We have been saving up and I'm delighted to tell you that next July, we will be travelling to California for three weeks' reunion with the American side of the family'.*

Mum adds: *'It's the perfect time for you two,'* and she looks at Sunny Jim and his sister, *'if you work hard for your big exams this summer, this will be the perfect reward'.*

Her face is delighted, any lingering memory of the moment Dad's pants caught fire is completely erased.

1971 is set to be a much happier year.

# Chapter 18: Gone (Dad #4)

One Monday early in June 2016, when we had been at the quest for over a year, we were sitting at the dining table wanting to speed things up. In front of us were Dad's 1971 diary, the manila "Divorce" file and lots of old letters from Mum.

I summarised the position Sunny Jim had reached: fifteen years old and disillusioned. The optimistic announcement about a family holiday in California was hardly going to remove Dad's underlying problems at home or at work. His three hammer blows (the house move, the estuary and the "revelation") had left the family reeling. Dad yearned to rip up all the miserable rules and build a better society. His religious beliefs were bringing him into conflict with colleagues at work and were not exactly compatible with the secular idealism of the Human Potential Movement. Dad was losing the plot. But the therapy of Doktor Spiel and the mentoring of Pieter Krakow had only buried him deeper into confusion and misery. No wonder he was moody and looking sick.

How could Dad possibly clear up the mess?

I ran through the next scenes with Helen, as calmly as I could, while inwardly seething with emotion.

*

- **Settings:** Rochester. 1971 Priestfields. Bull Ring cinema. Belle Tout Lighthouse
- **Props:** Monty Python. Bob and Carol etc
- **Characters:** Helen. Mum. Dad. Pieter Krakow and Brian Marshall and "Cal". Tutor.

With the Sixties over, its supercharged optimism is burning itself out. The Vietnam War has decimated a generation. Students have torn up the Paris streets, and popular protests have been violently quashed by the authorities. The Beatles are breaking up, and "Sympathy for the Devil" by the Rolling Stones signals a more sinister tone. Sunny Jim's household is stocking up with candles for government-imposed power blackouts. Factories are cutting down to three days a week. There are IRA bombs. One state of emergency follows another. Apollo 13 explodes.

In January 1971, Dad at 15 stone is badly overweight, but his morning exercise regime, described at the front of his diary, is rarely followed. Sunny Jim sits next to Dad on the sofa, while Dad is laughing like a drain at the Monty Python sketches in a desperate attempt to cheer himself up.

There are arguments raging late at night. Mum is saying: *'Look at yourself, bloated from business lunches with greedy managers. You pretend to be helping people but you're hardly a ragged trousered philanthropist!'* Mum fires long words at Dad: *'grandiose'*, *'solipsistic'*, *'egocentric'* and *'megalomaniac'*. Sunny Jim looks the words up afterwards. When Mum defeats Dad in the argument, he says: *'That hardly warrants a reply'*.

Dad is reporting nightmares. He is in poor shape, physically mentally and emotionally. Sunny Jim and his sister take him to Priestfields, a big open sports ground, for early morning runs. They're trying to repair him, but he needs more than a run round the block. He's a worn out car: his engine is lumpy, his steering and brakes unreliable. Dad is far from a fully functioning exemplar of the Human Potential Movement. He is needy and silently screaming for help.

One day in June 1971, Sunny Jim is once again in the car driving somewhere with Dad, who in a new spirit of openness is telling Sunny Jim about the night he and Pieter watched a film together at the Bull Ring in Birmingham: "Bob and Carol and Ted and Alice" about a so-called "Encounter Group" during an intense weekend on the cliff top at Esalen, California. Two couples openly discuss their sexual feelings, and contemplate swapping partners.

Dad tells Sunny Jim the astounding story Pieter told him in the bar after the film. When he gets home, an astonished Sunny Jim writes Pieter's story down.

### Pieter's story after showing Dad the Bob and Carol etc film
*When Brian Marshall and I were forming MKA, we got on well as a foursome too. One night at Brian's house in the London suburbs, one G&T led to another, but everyone was a little tense.*

*It was just like the Bob and Carol etc film.*

*We were trying to talk about our feelings towards one another, as if it was an Encounter Group. I felt desire towards Brian's wife, but I was afraid to say so. Why did I feel fear?*

*Then we had a choice: we could suppress these feelings, or go further to express them. But we couldn't just leap in. We had to agree to cross that boundary, or not to go there at all.*

*By nine pm, we had started to confess all kinds of desires towards one another accompanied with tearful emotions. After a couple of hours, our agreement was each to express these desires fully and directly, just for one night, to our colleague's wife. Brian offered his house, but to avoid an awkward scene at breakfast, I took Brian's wife back to my home.*

*Until that night Jenny was the wife of Brian, but that night we swapped and we didn't dare go back. Since then the wives refuse to see one another.*

*

I read out Sunny Jim's note to Helen and her eyes bulged. We continued.

*

Sunny Jim is in the front passenger seat hearing Pieter's story from Dad, glancing across at him to check he's heard correctly. Dad's frown is deeply set, and his left eye is twitching. Was Dad giving Sunny Jim a moral lesson against partner-swapping? No, because Dad admits his admiration for those people in the film who are living *'so openly, less shackled to the conventions of marriage'.* Clearly, Dad is interested in partner-swapping. Strangely, Dad is talking to Sunny Jim like client to counsellor, and he's showing obvious signs of distress.

Sunny Jim isn't a counsellor and doesn't know what to say. So he asks Dad to explain why Pieter took him to see the film. After a long moment Dad answers: *'I've always had difficulty putting myself in someone else's shoes. I assume Pieter wanted me*

*to understand why, despite those two being business partners, they no longer socialise and Pieter no longer works directly with Brian'.*

At Dad's next mentoring with Pieter Krakow, they're planning to hold an Esalen-style Encounter Group, similar to that depicted in the "Bob and Carol and Ted and Alice" film. Pieter invites Dad to bring Mum. When Mum declines the invitation, Dad attends the Group on his own. It takes place in a striking white lighthouse called Belle Tout, positioned on a white cliff west of Eastbourne and decommissioned due to being too high up for its light to save ships from the rocks below.

*

I showed Helen Dad's diary, which describes in March 1971 the lighthouse weekend:

**Friday:** *I looked forward to this Encounter group led by the tutor from Esalen, California. The village of East Dean was dark but it was not difficult to find Belle Tout standing high on the cliff. I arrived at 8.30pm, in time for supper and bed.*

**Saturday:** *An ecstatic day of silence. The tutor's reputation preceded him so no one argued about his strange instructions. We entered a pitch-black room, milling around, bumping into each other and noticing our ways of defending or invading the space and how we cling on.*

*I found Cal, my partner for the day. I walked blind-fold in her care. Marvellous sensations: rapturous, trustful joy, all in silence. She watched while I read, painted, and sculpted in clay. Then we swapped and I watched her.*

*Our evening sessions were intimate. We danced to music from Camelot. We described who we are, and the feelings we experienced. We "took off our masks", giving and getting feedback. We worked on our "problems" in a personal and emotional way, including massages, hugs and long walks in the dark.*

**Sunday:** *Cal was in the psychodrama where we acted out our father figures, pushing out our chests, striding, arms swinging, feet stamping. We "channelled" our domineering fathers by squaring up, bumping stomachs, grabbing lapels, and forcing each other to the ground.*

*One father pretended to show off a pretty lady. Another tripped over obstacles. One was smiling benignly. Another shoulders hunched, as if nose to a grindstone. But none was looking after any children, or cooking or chatting with family and friends. This was the "father archetype".*

*The "father mime" triggered feelings deep inside. I was invited to express these feelings through a skit, choosing someone to play father and another to play me. I placed them in position and left them to free expression. My father moved towards the child and away, coming and going from home to work. The child showed terror and howled as father approached, and subsided when he moved away. By the end the child was making piercing screams.*

*I watched rapt, then welled up. It was a relief. My father was so critical and demanding. On departure I felt an astonishing sense of love and gratitude towards Cal.*

Helen asked: *'What happened next?'* We moved on to the next scene.

*

- **Settings:** Oxford Street. Regent's Park. Rochester.
- **Props:** LPs of "Enigma Variations" and "Camelot".
- **Characters:** Dad. Cal. Mum.

The day after the lighthouse, Dad phones Cal and learns that *'she still cares'*. They arrange to meet the following week in a coffee bar. Cal arrives at that meeting with a female chaperone called Ruth, who leaves after an hour. Dad and Cal catch a bus to Oxford Street where they buy an LP ("Enigma Variations" and "Camelot"), then take a taxi to Regent's Park. It's not clear what happens there, but in the evening Dad and Cal go for an *'intimate meal'* in the Swiss Centre.

Dad catches the 11 o'clock train home. When he arrives Mum smells alcohol and suspects something. They stay up late talking, and in the morning Mum is tearful.

*

I asked Helen: *'How are we to interpret these events?'* During the ensuing discussion this is what we came to realise.

An intense correspondence was initiated by Mum while Dad was still at the Lighthouse, with this letter:

*Darling D*
*Writing this is terrifying because of the risks of exposing treacherous undercurrents in our marriage, but I do so in our new spirit of openness. I have to tell you that recently a penny has dropped: we are on the brink of failure, and I want to do whatever I can to save things...*

Mum was tired of worrying about Dad's life, and his many *'outside interests'*. She felt she had failed as a wife, and that was why he was seeking a *'perfect relationship'* elsewhere. Mum invited Dad's viewpoint on their marriage.

After a serious late-night talk on a *'tricky subject'*, with tears, Dad reported *'sweetness and light'* with a new understanding. Meanwhile, in the background, he was continuing to phone Cal towards a special meeting on 24th March, which looked like a date. When Dad returned home after that "date" with Cal, Mum confronted him, and Dad explained: it never was a date, simply a *'role-play with a third party'*, designed to include Mum's favourite things ("Enigma Variations" by Elgar, a walk in Regent's Park where they used to meet, and an intimate meal), in order to rekindle the affection in their marriage. Mum and Dad stayed awake much of the night discussing this "date".

At breakfast the morning after the fake date, Mum was tearful. That afternoon at work, Dad fell asleep in the midst of a meeting. That night, Mum and Dad slept together, and Dad's diary entry was triumphant: *'broke through sex barrier'*.

A letter from Cal to Dad on 30th March 1971 belied the innocence of Dad's tale about the "date". Cal's words in the letter were poetic and revealing: *'We have looked into one another's eyes and beyond. You have held me and felt the rhythm of my body'*. She expressed her delight at contributing to Dad's *'feeling freer and on better terms with your wife'*. But Cal was also confused: embarrassed at Dad's *'strong feelings'* towards her, while touched by this, but unwilling to upset her husband who felt threatened by Dad's interest in her.

On discovering that the Lighthouse weekend was the incubator for such strong feelings between Cal and Dad, I checked out the risks known to Carl Rogers the instigator of the Encounter Group method: *'The close and loving feelings which develop may become a source of threat and marital difficulty when a wife, for example, has not been present, but projects (her) fears about the loss of her spouse – whether well-founded or not – onto the workshop experience'*.

Rogers' description of the workshop aftermath closely fitted what Mum and Dad were living through. Mum may have been unaware of Cal's letter, or the feelings Cal and Dad were experiencing, but we can be sure she was suspicious. Her next letter confirmed that Dad was pressing her for permission to pursue an outside relationship. Mum's response began with tolerance and understanding: *'I do not resent these outside interests and recognise that you need them'*. She underlined the importance of the bond between them: *'My need is to be committed to one person, but for what it is worth, please feel as free as you can to do what you feel "right", knowing that I do not want to reject you whatever happens'*. She was giving him carte blanche.

In the middle of April, Dad wrote a page of what he called a *'theory of interpersonal relations'* with a circular diagram depicting how magnets induce electricity, and an explanation of how feelings in a married couple can be heightened by the proximity of a third person. He sent it to Mum for comment.

This time Mum's response was angry: *'In all your soul-searching I have been blamed for all your failures. I too have experienced the questionings of old values and reacted against the rigidity of the church. But there was not a time when I could take down my defences and admit this, because you did not appreciate I was in the same need of reassurance as I have given to you'*.

Mum went on to set out the benefits of marriage, the meaning of their vows and the boundaries they should place on any outside relationships, with the likely dangers of entering sexual relationships outside the marriage. This was Mum's defence against Dad's "Theory of Interpersonal Relations", against the prospect of his proposing further triangular relationships such as with Eve or Cal, and against the chance that Dad would try to bring her together with another couple a la Bob and Carol. Mum, who had been tolerant of Dad's outside relationships, was saying enough: *'You know my view: marriage is not just a piece of paper. We made vows to one another. I have no interest in further intimate relationships'*.

Dad took a different view: *'Rules are made to be broken!'* He wanted to be free.
Mum told Dad he was not free, because his presence was still required *'in critical moments during our day-to-day family life'*.

When I re-read the four letters from Cal to Dad, I could tell that she and her husband were refusing Dad's advances. Dad had been angling to draw Cal and her husband into an unconventional relationship.

A totally unexpected event put an end to this chapter. Towards the end of May, in the midst of her A level exams, my sister began to get pains in her legs, which were waking her up at night. From 2nd June through to the end of July, she was in and out of hospital, while her condition was getting more serious.

These tragic developments brought my parents, who had been at loggerheads, together for hospital visits each day.

That summer, me and my brothers went on holiday to America as planned, but with an Aunt and Uncle while our parents stayed at home to look after our sister. Soon after The Boys returned, our sister died.

*

Helen looked sad, and my head was bursting with complaints about Dad. He was a grown-up who regressed to a child and smashed everything up. When he was in a corner, he lied to everyone around him, and to himself. He was totally mixed up about religion and sex. He presumed to preach and tangled us up in his nonsense. We were his collateral damage, but he went on denying there was any such damage.

All of a sudden, I needed to get away. I put in my ear pods and selected "Day of Wrath" from Verdi's Requiem and ran out of the house towards the river. The music belting out from a large choir sent a chill rippling through my body. It was to do with Judgement Day, when sinners are said to be cast into eternal flames.

The savage beauty of that music brought out my anger: anger with myself for being naïve, anger with Dad for hiding the truth, and anger at Dad's lifelong lack of remorse. I was incandescent because no one understood and no one cared.

I went early to bed with questions spinning around my head. Everything good had been broken to pieces, plunging my once happy family into tragedy. "Gone Dad" entered my nightmare that night, driving dangerously, because I was driving towards him with my headlights dazzling and sending him out of control. His headlights were also shining on me, and I couldn't see the road any more. He was making me crash... I awoke in a sweat.

# Chapter 19: Vienna

A Tuesday arrived early in June 2016, the day after my angry run to Verdi's Requiem and I was ready for something restorative.

I was on an early morning flight to Vienna, listening to piano music by Debussy. It helped me reflect. I had an idea about how to understand Dad's destructive behaviour. The day ahead was free time, with no client work until the following morning. I would take things easy in Vienna and pay a visit to the Sigmund Freud Museum.

Who better, I thought, than the world's most famous psychologist, to cast light onto what rips a family apart? Sigmund Freud, the doctor who tried to heal his patients' conflicted minds, started the fashion for therapy, and fuelled a twentieth century obsession with "self at the expense of others": the century of Narcissism.

The flight to Vienna took just over two hours. The airport bus took me Schwedenplatz, and Hotel Graben was a short walk across the central shopping area. At the hotel, I dumped my bag and went straight out again.

It was a twenty minute walk to the museum at 19 Berggasse, the former home of Sigmund Freud. I wandered amongst his old furniture and mementos, including his unusual phallic ornaments, his first edition books and handwritten letters. I stopped to watch flickering film clips of his children and his constant family entourage. I stared at the couch where the great man's patients once recounted their dreams to his lurid interpretations. Freud was thinking the unthinkable, speculating towards ground-breaking insights, and writing prolifically. What drives us, he said, is ninety percent hidden, rather like an iceberg. Unconsciously, we play host to a monkey and a vicar, who jerk us around between the temptation of sex and the strictures of moral conscience. It's an endless war, hidden from view in the unconscious mind. Sex is so shameful he said, it has to be "sublimated" into approved activities, such as sport and religion. This fitted Dad.

The sun was shining as I sought out a place to enjoy the famous

Viennese coffee house tradition. Freud's favourite haunt, the Café Landtman with its deafening clatter was unsuitable for what I had in mind. I strolled on past the splendid Burgtheater, through the carefully laid out flowers of Volksgarten and the opulent Hofburg Palace. The city seemed beautiful and relaxed. It was hard to imagine the period of occupation by fascists, the allied bombing or people hiding in fear to escape being murdered. The peace and grandeur of the city were perfectly restored.

About 3pm, I arrived at Café Schwarzenberg, which dominated the corner of Ringstrasse and Kärntner. Booths lined the left-hand wall, hosting long friendly conversations over bratwurst and apfel strudel. I was lucky to nab an empty booth at the rear and slid behind a marble-topped table, which could have taken three people on either side.

The menu boasted *'you can surrender yourself completely'*. Each cup of coffee was delivered on its own silver tray with a glass of water. The staff were not particularly helpful, but this came with a benefit: they let you sit for hours in these coffee houses without bothering you.

I summoned a waiter dressed in black and white, and ordered goulash soup with brown bread. Fast food wasn't promised here, and that suited me. I settled in for a long wait. With my laptop connected to the Wi-Fi, I opened a folder of old family photographs. Flicking through the earlier generations with Grandpa and Grandma, Mum and Dad, aunts and uncles, brothers and sisters and cousins, I imagined conducting a bold experiment. I wanted to uncover the deeper reasons for what happened with Dad and, as it turned out, the afternoon produced some rather interesting results.

My plan was to listen carefully to certain family members, but in a special way: I would place myself in their shoes, and try to fathom the forces controlling them. I would be on the stove like a pot of soup, with the heat causing all sorts of deep material, unconscious and disowned feelings, to bubble to the surface. True, I would be working with named relatives but they would just be the representatives of my own inner conflicts. I wasn't going to criticise anyone and whatever came up would be about no one else but me.

The idea wasn't new. I had attended sessions with business teams using a method called Constellations, which assumes everyone is inter-connected and inter-dependent, and each person holds the power to make things better or worse for the others. Team members decide where to stand in a representation of the team: they move in and out, squaring up to or turning away from their peers, and words come to them. By exchanging these words, individuals can be released from tension, and team relations can continue with more clarity, vigour and joy. Long ago, I completed a professional training in the method, but I never dared explore the topics of Dad and family, because those matters were too personal.

Of course, I had no intention of standing up in the Café Schwarzenberg and putting on a big display. A year of working at my dining table had created a quieter alternative. I could use photographs as data and objects to represent the people. By moving them into position, I could provoke the responses. I would pay careful attention to everything, and write it all down.

When my goulash finally arrived, the waiter placed the bowl to my left, leaving a free space on my right. On my laptop in the middle, I displayed my tracing of a family photograph dated March 1957, showing Grandpa and Sunny Jim.

*

Grandpa, smartly dressed in suit and tie, is passing two-year-old Sunny Jim, a plate of food. This is their first contact because Grandpa is usually overseas in Austria (what a funny coincidence!) deep in post-war reconstruction and too distant to interfere.

Sunny Jim is reaching towards the cakes and can't resist the one with a cherry. There is a clear family rule you have to eat a sandwich before any cakes, but Sunny Jim is too young to know. Grandpa winks to Sunny Jim as if to say OK, and the small boy slips the cherry into his mouth.

*

This scene played out like a film in my mind, and between sips of goulash soup, I was remembering the action, visualising the characters and where they were standing, and writing it all down. When I hit a blank, I used the table to my right as the stage. I put an HP Sauce bottle (surprising to find in Vienna!) in position to represent Grandpa, and a pot of sugar for Sunny Jim.

While touching the pot of sugar, I felt with my own tongue the shape of the cherry in Sunny Jim's mouth. He hadn't swallowed it so he hadn't broken the rule, and technically he was in the clear.

*

Everyone is moving away in horror, leaving Sunny Jim isolated as

if under a spotlight. There is a line of three characters in the
shadows: Dad, Grandpa and Grandma. Grandma and Dad are
staring horrified at Sunny Jim, while Grandpa is going red in the
face.

*

After another sip of goulash, I moved Mum (represented by the
salt grinder) in towards centre-stage. I knew what she needed to
do.

*

Mum squats down to face Sunny Jim and says to him sternly: *'Did you take the cherry?'* She is aware of being watched from the shadows.

Sunny Jim shakes his head, and Mum reacts by fishing in his mouth, while the other three keep staring from the shadows. Mum retrieves the cherry, but her witnesses require more, so she says: *'That was very naughty. You took the cherry, and you lied to us. You must learn to tell the truth!'* She grabs Sunny Jim's hand and drags him into the garden. Dad follows. The grandparents watch approvingly from indoors.

Mum pulls down Sunny Jim's shorts and slaps him hard on the thigh. He cries. Mum hisses at Dad: *'Why didn't you step in?'* Dad looks across to Grandpa at the window, then back at Mum.

Then Mum and Dad retreat and leave Sunny Jim in the garden howling, until Grandma brings him back inside. She cuddles him and sings a song:

*Climb up on my knee, Sonny Boy*
*Though you're only three, Sonny Boy*
*You've no way of knowing*
*There's no way of showing*
*What you mean to me, Sonny Boy.*

Then he is fine again and Mum appears saying: *'Come along Sunny Jim'.* This is the first time he is called Sunny Jim.

*

I wrote it all down, wondering why Dad, a grown man in his thirties, was giving in to his parents, and offering up his own son to mollify them. Grandpa was wrong to offer Sunny Jim the cake, but he was hiding the mistake, and pushing for Sunny Jim to be smacked, in violation of Dad and Mum's agreed rule against such punishment.

Dad was caught in the middle between Mum and Grandpa, and Grandpa was driving a wedge between Mum and Dad. I needed to figure out why he was doing that.

By now, I'd finished the goulash soup and I ordered a beer. I was about to put myself in Grandpa's shoes.

*

Grandpa is the son of a Post Office supervisor, born in Islington, with four brothers and three sisters. In 1918 he is a returning hero after four long years in the bloodiest location, The Somme, of the bloodiest war, World War 1, and lucky because sixteen

million have recently lost their lives, and countless more have been deeply damaged. As a Despatch Rider, Grandpa carries messages on his motorbike through mud and barbed wire, from generals to the frontline. He learns the hard way that if we can communicate well and follow orders precisely, it's easier to win. This is how Grandpa's "good guys" can become the stronger force, and beat the "bad guys".

By the end, Grandpa and the good guys win and force Kaiser Wilhelm to abdicate. There is rioting in Germany, a mutiny in France, and a revolution in Russia. People everywhere are demanding the right to govern themselves. The women who kept the factories running are granted the vote and promised an equal voice. Ordinary people are no longer accepting orders, so those in command have no choice but to change how they run things.

Grandpa, with his sights set on promotion in the Civil Service, assembles a shelf of self-improvement books by William James, William Shakespeare and John Ruskin. The Dictionary of Musical Terms is on this shelf for another reason: to attract a young woman who plays hymns in his church. He asks her for piano lessons with this ulterior motive, and it works because in 1925 they marry. Over the next four years, Grandma and Grandpa produce three children. The first of these is Dad.

*

I remembered Auntie M's accounts of her childhood, and put three olives on the stage to represent the three children. I touched them briefly and waited for them to tell me their story.

*

Life in the 1930s recession isn't too bad for this young family, despite needing to move every three years with Grandpa's War Office assignments. When Dad is five, they are living in Egypt, and the family's happy experiences are captured in some charming photographs.

The three children play happily together. Dad, being the eldest and the boy, naturally is allowed to be the teacher and the vicar,

while his two younger siblings are content to play pupils and congregation.

"Grandpa's Code" is the key to family life for the three little olives. Grandpa says: *'The father is a Commanding Officer taking the decisions, and steering the family in the right direction, based on all available intelligence about the enemy and the lie of the land'.*

Grandpa tells Grandma her place too: *'The mother is Chief of Staff, running the family unit on a day-to-day basis, communicating the decisions, upholding standards and maintaining morale'.*

"Perfection" is assumed to be crucial by Grandma as an accomplished musician, and also by Grandpa as a surviving soldier. They both keep a sharp eye out for "imperfection" as measured by the seven deadly sins taught in church: anger, envy, gluttony, greed, hubris, lust, and sloth.

Often Grandpa is travelling, and the children are entertained at home by Grandma, who compensates them with cakes, ice creams and songs. Each time Grandpa returns, he senses the discipline at home is slackening. It is widely considered to be kinder-in-the-long-run to punish the child than to spoil them. Since discipline is not Grandma's strength, Grandpa, spurred on by the gathering clouds of war, toughens the regime at home.

Events come to a head, when in 1936 Italy annexes Ethiopia, and Hitler reoccupies Rhineland, in defiance of the League of Nations. It is a bleak disappointment for Grandpa that the last war did not bring an end to all wars, and it's becoming a stark fact that millions died in vain.

*

I remembered Uncle D telling me the famous phrase from Churchill that Grandpa offered him as parenting advice: *'Appeasement is like feeding a crocodile hoping it won't eat you in the end: it only speeds the enemy's advance'.*

*

When a child refuses his vegetables at dinner, Grandpa begins with charm and reasoning, but when these fail he puts the child over his knee. Hard slaps to the bare bottom are applied, with irregular pauses for the added torture of not-knowing whether another slap will arrive. Then the child is sent off to the bedroom, not to return until willing to eat all the vegetables.

*

I shuddered as that scene unfolded, and all of a sudden Dad's psychodrama in the lighthouse returned. There Dad, who claimed no memory of his childhood, remembered his inner child howling at the approach of his father. Next, into my mind came Grandpa.

*

Grandpa is flushed and, with eyes streaming and tears dripping from the end of his nose, he lands the blows. The other children sit still as statues, trying to stay out of the firing line.

*

Then I saw the face of the perpetrator changing. Grandpa became Dad. He was thrashing me for not eating my vegetables. I wrote this in my notes: *'Punishments spread down the generations'.*

*

Triggered by the slightest timidity or imperfection in his children, Grandpa's punishments increase, and to match this, so do the privileges. Under these "hothouse" conditions a child has no certainty about whether a beating, or an ice cream will arrive next. Grandpa wants to be loving, upright, kind and generous, after all he is a "good guy", but he also needs to toughen his children to withstand the troubles ahead. Grandpa's hothouse regime fails to produce the desired result and, at the age of ten, Dad is sent to a strict boarding school.

Three years later, the Second World War starts and Grandpa is away for six years in foreign parts. He returns with medals and commendations, to add to the merits he brought back at the age of twenty-two in 1918.

A generation later, Dad at twenty-two returns home empty-handed. It is 1948 and, after four years in the RAF, Dad confesses to Grandpa he has seen no action, and worse, he has crash-landed a plane by forgetting to lower the under-carriage. After he failed to graduate to pilot, he became bored, badly behaved and was no longer considered officer material. He asks Grandpa: *'How can I live up to your high expectations?'*

Grandpa's first tip is to look for "the perfect wife". Dad meets a girl at a company dance, becomes besotted, tries to buy her a ring but she refuses saying she doesn't love him. He doesn't give up. Six months later, he is at the Strand Palace Hotel introducing his new fiancée, Mum, to Grandpa and Grandma. The young couple are clearly in love, and they have taken the trouble to work out a plan for their marriage. Grandpa confirms his approval by writing a cheque for fifty guineas towards the wedding.

*

In the Café Schwarzenberg, the whole story was pouring through my mind, switching on the synapses like hot coffee. I re-opened the 1949 wedding photo on the laptop and re-positioned the condiments. In the centre I put the tall, black pepper grinder to represent Dad, and the smaller transparent salt grinder to be Mum, with the groom on the left, bride on the right. Grandma was represented by the olive oil jar on the left of Dad. Grandpa was the HP Sauce bottle some distance behind Dad. Mum's mother, Granny, was a silver cup of toothpicks to the right of Mum.

*

This time, I enter the scene and speak directly to Dad: *'What do you wish all the guests here to know?'*
Dad recoils momentarily, before delivering a squeaky-clean answer: *'That I am decent, respectable and worthy as a husband'.*

Dad discloses that under Grandpa's beady eye he has to ignore a devilish inner voice which tells him: *'Go on, just bunk off with your new wife and leave the guests to complete the formalities'.*

I ask Dad: *'What expectations do you sense from those surrounding you here?'*
Dad heaves a sigh, then with a grin he lifts up his hand and jokingly whispers to Mum: *'We are surrounded, between my mother and my new in-laws, and my father taking potshots from behind'.*

At this, Mum is giggling and shushing him. Grandma is nearby and bristling. She turns to face Mum and Dad, raising a discrete finger to her lips. Her quick glance back to Grandpa apologises for these giggly departures from protocol, and she recomposes herself ready for the next photograph.

I ask Mum: *'What would you wish those people surrounding you not to know?'*
She glances around to take in the company, then gives a considered response: *'I would not wish anyone here to know exactly what just arose in the last two minutes between me, my husband and his parents'.*
Mum sees that Dad is caught up, in what Maslow once called the "bonds of neurotic control", with complex feelings of failure, guilt

and shame emanating from his father and mother. Dad is over-shadowed by his parents.

*

I brought myself out of that scene, and on a whim I Googled Carl Jung. This famous Swiss psychologist and follower of Sigmund Freud, coined the term "shadow", and after a vivid dream he described it like this:

*'I was making slow headway against a mighty wind. My hands were cupped around a tiny light, which threatened to go out at any moment. Something was coming up behind: a gigantic black figure following me. But, in spite of my terror I had to keep the little light going.*

*'When I awoke I realised the figure was my own shadow on the swirling mists, brought into being by my little light. The little light was my consciousness, though infinitely small in comparison with the powers of darkness, it is my only light.'*

Jung told us not to ignore our shadows, even though they frighten us, because when ignored they grow in strength and threaten to destroy us. When we face up to our shadows, we brighten the light of our consciousness and it's much easier to go on living.

For the next scene I brought Mum and Dad to centre stage.

*

They are very happy because their five-year plan is working out well. Mum has passed her finals and is ready to begin working as a doctor. Dad's career is on track. They have bought their first home and have in just three years produced three of their (to be) four children.

Grandpa and Grandma are returning from overseas and they observe Mum and Dad. Grandma spots mistakes with the napkins and laundry. Grandpa sees a young wife struggling with the simple job of running a home, while stubbornly continuing her career. Even worse, the woman is left-leaning politically, and sceptical about religion. They see two young parents confused about their roles, slapdash with the chores and soft on the children. The husband is failing to exercise proper authority at home and, in Grandpa's view, a serious turnaround is required.

*

A wave of sadness crashed over me.

*

I re-enter the scene, and ask for Mum's point of view: *'Dad and I were united against the world, but Grandpa returned and Dad fell into a constant struggle between being a good partner to me, and a good son to his parents'.*

Mum adds damning details: *'Grandpa's advice was unsuited to our situation, as two working parents without servants to rely on. From our wedding day onwards, Dad was hyper-sensitive to his parents' criticism. He tried to be the perfect husband in the perfect marriage, but this was not remotely realistic. He wanted me to be the fantasy woman in the romantic films he watched during the war: constantly happy, excited, dedicated, uncomplaining and loyal, just like his doting mother, and without a mind of my own. I couldn't possibly live up to those standards of perfection'.*

Meanwhile, Dad's light of consciousness, as Jung would have said, is flickering against mighty winds. Dad is caught between Grandpa and Mum.

*'What was the consequence?'* I ask Mum.
She replies: *'Grandpa's campaign began covertly, and perhaps without malice. He lent Dad money to buy the car Dad craved (a Humber Super Snipe). I argued and refused to drive the car. Dad went to Grandpa for advice. Grandpa told him I was denying him the chance to make a mark on the world. Grandpa advised Dad to find a worthy cause and commit to it, something like the war. He said the rest of the family would soon adjust'.*

With Grandpa's undermining moves, the momentum is becoming unstoppable. Dad changes jobs, enrols in politics with the

Liberal Party, and the family moves house to Tonbridge. Dad is becoming a candidate in the local elections. Dad is getting involved with the evangelists at church. Dad is moving Granny in to the family house against Mum's wishes, so that he is freed up to continue making his mark outside.

By giving in to Grandpa, Dad is tearing up his agreements with Mum and, by the time Grandpa dies in 1960, it is too late. Rather than return to joint decisions, Dad becomes a Strict Dad, trying to be perfect. Later, when that hasn't worked, he becomes a Hippie bent on changing society. Filled with resentment, Mum refuses to join in.

By the late Sixties, when Dad discovers humanistic psychology, the marriage is already doomed. Dad is becoming narcissistic, obsessed with trying to change himself. He is battling against the "bindings of social control" around him. He fantasises that he is a pioneer, liberating people, creating families and "mini-societies" that will unleash human potential.

*

That Tuesday afternoon in the café, I watched Dad's life, once apparently dedicated to serving others, became all about his craving for acceptance, respect and happiness. The more he obsessed about becoming a free, creative and fully functioning person, the less acceptance, respect and happiness he received.

As I walked back to the Hotel Graben, I reflected on the afternoon I'd spent in the booth at the cafe, and my grandparents' part in Dad's misfortune. I remembered a line from a poem: *'the child is father of the man'.* Upbringing is important, I decided, but how much can we blame on our parents, and on our genes? Isn't it up to us to play the cards we're dealt?

Once back in my hotel room, I should have been preparing for my client meeting the following day. But Dad's Human Potential Movement was weighing on my mind. His involvement with that Movement reduced the rest of us to bit players in a drama that was all about him.

## Chapter 20: Surreal Adventure Reprise

With my head on the pillow in the Graben Hotel that Tuesday
night in June 2016, something shifted in me and I no longer
wanted the artifice of "theatre director", "Sunny Jim" and "stage".
Mentally, I stepped fully in, owning up myself to being the
sixteen-year-old star of the drama. With this shift, more of the
story came back to me.

1971 was a disastrous year. I now know that during the happiest
summer of my young life, while we were travelling up Highway
One, through Big Sur in California, we passed the entrance to
Esalen, the centre of the Human Potential cult that was driving
Dad crazy. But Dad was not with us, he was with Mum looking
after our dying sister in hospital. This wonderful holiday, during
which I experienced freedom, infatuation and heartbreak (I'll
not say more), only added to the widening gulf when we arrived
home.

Everyone was sinking in sorrow and despair during my sister's
final days. How could a family bridge those extremes of
happiness and sorrow? The Boys were decent enough to muffle
their joy while Mum was crying in the chair, but the situation was
miserable and confusing. How could I help anyone? How could
I help myself? I had lost touch with my feelings. When my sister
died that September, I wanted someone or something to blame.
I rejected the church, and I harboured suspicions about Dad and
whatever he was mixed up in at work. But I got on with life, going
to school and refusing to be distracted.

The autumn rolled by. Christmas was sad. I went out often and
spent time with friends, rather than sink into the gloom at home.
Childish I suppose. I wrote letters to a girl in California. I watched
the film of Woodstock and yearned to be there.

In the summer of 1972, the edifice of a childhood came crashing
down during the trip to Germany with Dad in the white camper
van, an event that I had previously tried to discuss with my
brothers. Dad's 1972 diary left out all the important bits, not
least the fact that I returned a different person.

Earlier that summer, Dad said something strange to me in the car: *'I've done something terrible. I've slept with another woman'.* His knotted face told me this was complicated: *'The trouble is when you sleep with a woman you become morally obliged to marry her'.* That part was misleading and incorrect, so I said: *'Really?'* We both let the matter drop and it went right out of my mind.

When Saturday 29th July 1972 arrived, we set off in the morning sunshine. Dad was driving our white Fiat Fiesta camper van, with Mum sitting beside. A light atmosphere suggested they had patched things up, after the terrible year in which my sister died. I was two months into being seventeen, and sitting in the back with my thirteen-year-old brother. My other brother was away on some activity, musical I think, and our sister left a big gap too. On the roof, eight blue bungee straps radiating from a chrome ring held down nine cardboard boxes that Dad called the "Blocks to Creativity".

The surprises began in Dover. Mum got out at the station with no explanation, and took the train home. Our six green bottles were down to three, but with Dad only half there, it was really two and a half.

At Ostend, the approaching cars hooted at us to drive on the right. Dad, his face set in a frown, was gripping the wheel, trance-like. He kept the speed down to 50 miles per hour, without slowing for roundabouts and traffic lights. Fierce last-minute braking was sometimes needed to save our lives.

I sat in the front like a hostage trying desperately to engage my captor: *'What will be happening when we get to the summer school?'* We knew it was called a summer school but Dad wasn't sharing any vital details. I hoped for fun and adventure, other families, teenagers, and possibly girls. Any questions were dismissed curtly: *'You'll have to wait and see'.* My brother in the back was silent, and I gave up too.

It was hot without aircon, so we rolled down the windows: this was noisier, and not much cooler. The hours drifted by in silence. That night we camped, I'm not sure where, and we set off driving again early on Sunday. Mid-afternoon Dad stopped to sleep. My brother and I wandered around grumpily. After a long time Dad woke up, got out a map, rotated it, looked up at the sun, then silently made up his mind how to go forward.

Silently we continued the journey, and to myself I critiqued Dad's steering, braking and indicating. I would have been happy to navigate. We were bored, bored, bored. There were no games and nothing to occupy us, except to take turns keeping an eye on Dad, while the other one slept in the back.

At three in the morning, under a starry moonlit sky, we arrived at a place high in the mountains. Dad let us into a silent house and took us up to a bedroom with two beds. He left us alone to sleep. I felt relieved but exhausted.

It's not so easy to explain what happened for the rest of that week. Later that Monday morning, we awoke hungry in an unfamiliar, empty house, the sun streaming in. We dressed and went looking for breakfast, and Dad. We walked past closed doors, down the stairs, where the familiar outline of our camper van through a stained glass front door was a small reassurance. Once outside, I glanced back at the house: gothic and turreted, with an ornate timbered conservatory wrapped around. Manicured lawns sloped down towards distant forested hills.

A clattering of plates drew us towards a second fine house beyond the grass. Thirty or forty people were scattered over several small tables on a sprawling sunlit terrace. As we approached, their chatting, in English with a mix of accents, French, German and American, sounded happy but oddly intense, as if something momentous was due to occur.

My brother spotted Dad first, chatting in a small group on a distant table, looking relaxed and unlike the frowning man who drove us here. We stood by his table waiting and he turned with a feeble smile: *'Ah you found us. Breakfast is over there, just help yourselves. Our meeting is about to start, so I'll see you afterwards at lunchtime'.*

Breakfast didn't take long. There were stewed plums, yoghurt, nuts and muesli. We called it hippie food. The couple serving, with navy blue dungarees and long hair, had nothing we recognised, no cornflakes or toast.

We had to find out where we were. We moved despondently along corridors, up and down staircases, and past closed doors, finding nothing to grab us during a rough inspection of the two houses. We wandered across lawns, into woods, and down a hill to a lake. Time dragged.

At lunchtime, Dad was on the terrace again, looking unusually at ease with those around him. We complained about the food, and he dismissed this breezily: *'It's macrobiotic, and very good for you'.* He let us eat alone, then disappeared for the afternoon, leaving us once more to entertain ourselves.

It could have been paradise. The sky was so blue and the setting so beautiful. But we had run out of ideas. I unbuttoned my shirt and lay down on a grassy bank to sunbathe. My brother perched uncomfortably beside me.

I awoke to the sound of scrunching sandals on a gravel path above. I rolled onto my front and on raising my head spied two men approaching: stark naked. I ducked down and shut my eyes, then cautiously looked again to find a crowd of naked adults milling on the grass, chatting in pairs and small groups, unembarrassed about their lumpy physiques.

But my young brother had disappeared.

Self-consciously amidst that scene of nudity, I re-buttoned my shirt and moved stealthily through shrubs towards the turreted house. My brother was in the bedroom on his back, with a pillow on his face: I pulled it off.
He said: *'Did you see them?'*
I said: *'Yes. What shall we do?'*

We both said: *'I'm not taking off my clothes'.*
He said: *'So why are they naked?'*
We shrugged.

It wasn't the nakedness, but the uncertainty this cast over what might happen next. How we reacted is the interesting part. The adults, preoccupied with themselves, were casting off their clothes. We didn't understand. We had no wish to conform either. We began asking ourselves: why should we play by the rules, when the adults aren't? We let ourselves off the leash too.

This brought a spring to our steps. We strode back purposefully into the houses and explored thoroughly this time, opening the closed doors to find valuables: car keys, wallets and passports. We were burglars, and giggly with it. But we didn't take anything.

We found the adults' meeting room that previously we'd considered out of bounds. There were circles of beanbags instead of chairs, and no tables at all. The "Blocks to Creativity" were lined up at the side, open with papers spilling out. The floor was strewn with discarded clothes. Through the French windows naked adults were still strolling across the lawns, not seeing us.

Even when we moved outside, no one noticed. As dressed people, we were invisible and we didn't matter. We strolled happily in anonymity, no longer seeking answers, just for the joy of discovery. Inside the second house we found a "dumb waiter" lift in a kitchen, with a *'Menschen Verboten'* sign. We disobeyed, and took turns to squeeze into the forbidden lift, riding up and down between the floors.

The hot sunny days passed easily, in a happy blur. We went to the furthest edges of the thirty-nine hectare estate, returning only for meals and sleep. On the Tuesday, far from the main houses, we came across a red brick building set in a hillside. It was locked and despite all efforts we failed to break in. This gave us our mission for the next day.

On the Wednesday, we approached the house from the hill at the back, and my smaller brother pushed himself in through the first floor window, releasing a door to let me in. We found a boss's office, and took turns to swing in a buttoned-leather chair. With a guilty thrill, we imagined ourselves in charge. We rifled through drawers in a big desk to find black-edged envelopes, and a small bottle of Underberg, but we didn't drink it.

What was this place? Trying to imagine made our offence seem serious. We had broken in to someone else's world and there was a risk of getting caught.

We went downstairs into a large room, with benches and fume cupboards, conical flasks, condensing flasks, distillation apparatus, clamps and Bunsen burners; just like at school. Shelves had lines of chemicals in bottles with ground glass stoppers labelled hydrochloric and sulphuric, potassium and phosphorous. The drawers had fresh books of litmus paper and unopened packets of glossy Kodak paper.

When we figured out this was a small well-stocked science lab in a privileged school, we laughed with excitement. Then shushing with the terror of being discovered, we went over what we had done, and what might happen. We hadn't taken or broken anything, except for some pointless rules. We were simply authorising ourselves, like the naked adults, and with this thought we felt confident and entitled. No adult was there to tell us any different. We were invisible and beyond the reach of the law.

In whispers over breakfast on Thursday, our next plan came together. It was never a conscious revenge on the adults, just a tacit tit-for-tat. We would purloin what we liked from the lab. We spent the morning listing what to take, and thinking about how. That afternoon we were in the lab, checking through our list and weighing up how to proceed. We kept wavering and altering our positions. One of us was beaming with excitement saying: *'It's a*

*victimless crime. No one is using this. No one comes here any more'.*
The other suddenly was the voice of caution saying: *'No, everything belongs to someone, this school is only closed for summer'.*

Neither of us wanted to get into trouble. While one saw layers of dust and spiders' webs as proof that years had passed since a lesson, the other imagined police arriving with guns, and being thrown in jail. We ended up polarised that day, with one brother for committing the crime (*'because no one will ever find out'*), and the other refusing to help.

The next day was Friday, and the cautious one relented. We were in it together again. We borrowed Dad's keys, and stealthily stashed the hoard under seats in the camper. Dad, still with his head in the clouds, could never find out.

The sky darkened late that afternoon, and blistering white flashes lit up the treetops on the mountainsides around us. We found the adults gathering fully clothed in the conservatory of the second house, and joined them in counting down the seconds before each rumble arrived. We were tracking the approach of a ferocious storm. It felt biblical, as if God was punishing all the adults' foolish antics (this despite my being a declared atheist for over a year).

The lightning struck overhead, with an ear-splitting crack, then the heavens gave up the first heavy drops. Thick torrents of water washed down the windows, masking our view. We withdrew from the darkness outside, and moved deeper inside the house. Dinner was served indoors, after which my brother left in heavy rain for our bedroom in the other house. I stayed up with the adults. With a bright fire in the hearth, we sang songs late into the night.

A young American girl taught me to fingerpick a guitar tune called "Let It Rain". I saw Dad watching me with that girl, the fire glowing in her face. Late that night, the rain had stopped and I walked over drenched lawns to my bed feeling very happy. I was no longer adrift. At last I belonged. I slept with that girl, in my dreams.

At lunch on Saturday, Dad was saying goodbye to everyone. For the first time that week he had something to say to us: *'We are leaving tomorrow'*.

An American butted in to ask Dad a question: *'When are you coming back?'*
Dad replied: *'In one week's time, next Saturday'*.
I was taken aback.
The American's next question was disturbing: *'Are you bringing your girlfriend?'*
I assumed some mistake, until Dad replied: *'Yes'*.
Then I was pulsing with anger because Dad was two-timing Mum.

Casually, Dad returned to our arrangements: *'Make sure you are packed and ready to leave tomorrow after lunch'*.
It was a surprise to me when I replied: *'No, I'll be staying a few more days, and making my own way home'*. I said it quite calmly, and Dad didn't resist, but I didn't yet know how I'd get home. Later that day, a Belgian family agreed to drive me to Brussels in a few days' time, because they wanted me to babysit their daughter.

So the camper van went before me with our secret hoard. My brother unloaded it stealthily into the cellar at home. I was driven to Brussels, and from there I caught a train to Ostend, then the ferry and a train home from Dover.

As I approached home, I was sure Dad would be normal again. It was always the same after a scary scene calmed down. Family life went on. No one said anything. But I felt different this time, because I had taken matters into my own hands.

By the time school resumed that September, I no longer wanted to be at home. I protested by smoking cigarettes and drinking in pubs with my friends, in the full knowledge Dad disapproved, celebrating secretly because he couldn't stop me.

Dad told Mum about Shirley, and that she was pregnant. At that time, Mum was slumped in the armchair and crying a lot, but soon she woke up and gave Dad an ultimatum: he had to choose. Dad offered a third alternative he called *'peaceful co-existence'*. Mum and Shirley met to discuss what this might mean, but nothing came of it, and Dad still had to choose.

The morning after Mum's meeting with Shirley was Sunday 8th October 1972. We were sitting in what used to be my sister's bedroom, where twelve months earlier we sat dividing my sister's possessions: her guitar went to me, her coin collection to one brother and her room to the other brother.  This time Mum and Dad were breaking more bad news: their trial separation, but it should only be temporary they said. I didn't believe them.

A few days later, I was pushing open the back gate after school, to find Dad carrying boxes to a hired van. He had tools from the cellar, clothes from the wardrobe, and files from his office. I ignored him. Why should I help? It was his decision to leave.

He asked me to hold open the gate. I did so without a word. He put a last load in the van and then said this: *'You're the eldest now. The others need you to take responsibility'.*

Those words were strangely provocative. I was bursting inside, just as in Germany when Dad's two-timing was exposed. A voice in my head screamed: *'Like you are taking responsibility? After being "so perfect" all these years? That is your space to fill not mine'.*

I should have confronted him, but I didn't. I stayed silent. A strong inner protector took charge and noted three outrageous new demands: you need to fill the shoes of your dead sister; fill Dad's shoes; and look after your brothers.

My silence had an effect and Dad moved to justify himself: *'All these years, I have fulfilled my responsibilities when all I ever really wanted was to run away and play'.*

This from Dad was more than just a feeble excuse: it was from the heart, the heart of a small boy. I didn't want to lose my Dad, although he was letting us down badly. I told myself a father is for life. Anxiously I blurted out: *'I no longer need a father, so can't we be friends instead?'*

He agreed, and it was a bad bargain, because after that my relations with Dad became more confused and bothersome.

# Chapter 21: Misnomers

I awoke early on the Wednesday morning in June 2016 in Hotel Graben, with a workday in front of me, and belatedly completed the necessary client prep.

When I went down to breakfast, I carried a single and unrelated thought: that "friendship" with Dad was a misnomer. A better word was "collusion". What pretended to be a sensible adjustment left us both short-changed: Dad no longer needed to act responsibly towards his son, and I no longer needed to respect him as a father. After tearing up the obligations we presumed were out-dated, we set a confused tone for subsequent events, bordering on role reversal, at times bringing me to fury.

With a taxi due to arrive at 10am to take me to the client meeting, I gave myself one full hour to write the briefest summary of those events.

*

Dad moved out of our family home in October 1972, but shortly afterwards we heard that he and Shirley were arguing and she had a miscarriage. That autumn, I saw Granny in her room in our house with eyes red from crying, and debris strewn around her on the floor as she scribbled over Dad's face with blue biro and snipped him out of her family photos.

I entered 1973 with Dad trying to entice me into meeting Shirley, but I didn't want to know. He promised to buy me a car for my eighteenth, and he said cars were cheaper in the north. I visited the Buxton house he shared with Shirley and we hunted down an Austin 1100 for £70. I drove the banger home to Rochester and put it through an MOT, but it failed. A few days' later I returned it to Buxton.

That September, Dad was visiting Rochester for long discussions with Mum. He wanted to unite the two families into a "mini-society". He was trying to sell me on his plan: *'many hands make light work, we can all live under one roof'* etc. It was supposed to be a fresh start with fewer rules and a happier mood. He said

lots of families would soon be living like this. I wasn't convinced.
I imagined Dad sneaking in the darkness between Mum's and
Shirley's beds and at breakfast we would all be sitting there, Mum
and Shirley and The Boys, with a big silly smile on Dad's face.

Dad's next step was to invite us to a meeting in Tunbridge Wells
for *'everyone in the family'*, in which he included Shirley and her
son from a previous relationship. I erupted at Dad: *'Do The Boys
want to live in your "mini-society"? No, obviously we don't! Do
we want your other woman under our roof? No, and obviously
Mum doesn't either. You've messed things up, so sort it out with
Mum. Stop asking us!'*

Mum did go to the meeting with Shirley, but The Boys refused.
She returned tearful, and said: *'Shirley is pregnant again and
I'm worn out, I can't keep this going'*. She wrote Dad a long
letter explaining why everyone said *'no'* to what she called his
*'eternal triangle'*, and she agreed to grant him the divorce he was
seeking.

Meanwhile, Dad's daily arguments with Shirley were draining
him. They moved from Buxton to Sheffield just before Christmas.
The baby was born in March 1974. It was not Dad's long sought
"perfect relationship". He complained that Shirley was jealous
and insecure. Dad was suffering because he couldn't quite get
the old family out of his mind. Dad went for "rebirthing therapy"
(more on this soon) believing it might give him a fresh start.

That summer, with two years of trial separation completed,
the recently reformed divorce law allowed for solicitors to be
engaged and legal papers to begin moving to and fro.

My bothers and I did not expect Dad to return home in
December 1974, as if the two years of separation and the
new family had never happened. Mum and Dad's divorce was
suddenly off and it was reconciliation time. Dad tried to slot
back in as if he still belonged: sitting down to Christmas dinner,
entertaining the neighbours and visiting relatives. But The Boys
did their best to ignore him.

For the next three months, Dad flitted between his new family
in Sheffield and his old family in Rochester, and his diary

references to *'breakfast in bed'* suggested he was sharing
bedrooms with both women.

*

I glanced at the image of a familiar letter on my laptop:

*29 April 1975*

*Dear D*

*I have just spent the evening turning round all the furniture in the
lounge and doing a lot of thinking.*

*However hard I tried to be "a good wife" nothing would make my
personality match yours. You were struggling with this fact for all
our married life. I came to enjoy who you were rather than hope
for you to be different, and I hoped you would come to enjoy
marriage with me as I am. Now I understand that you cannot
and this made me want to free you from our marriage.*

*During today's furniture reorganisation I noticed so much we
worked at and shared, and whatever your relationship becomes
with Shirley, I don't want to make you feel uneasy about coming
here. Please feel free to visit, without pressure to stay or change
your way of living.*

*With love, N*

This letter was Mum's charming way of saying: *'I've reinstated
our divorce proceedings'.*

*

That summer Dad left the country for Kenya, on a three-year
contract, with Shirley and the two new sons.

The divorce was granted on 5th January 1976. That autumn,
Dad visited me in Bristol where I was an unemployed graduate.
He didn't find out how unhappy I was, because he monopolised
us with his quandary about leaving Shirley to return to Mum. He
was in distress because Mum refused to take him back. I later
learned that Mum's relatives advised her to refuse Dad. Uncle D

told her to bash Dad hard on his head with a frying pan to bring him to his senses. I felt no sympathy and told Dad it was over with Mum and there were plenty more fish in the ocean.

In 1977, Dad returned to Shirley and they married. Helen and I attended their wedding.

In 1984, work brought me to a Brighton Hotel and I invited Dad to visit me there. It was after his divorce from Shirley and shortly before his third wedding. It seemed a perfect moment to ask him a few heartfelt questions.

I met him in the hotel foyer. The bar was crowded and noisy so we went up to my room where it would be easier to talk. I made a cup of tea, and my stomach was clenched as I summoned every ounce of courage to ask the big question I assumed we both needed the answer to: *'Why did the family break up?'*

Dad stared back in stunned silence, and the blood rose to his face.
I felt like an impertinent child, due for a punishment.
He delayed with a question: *'Which one?'*

I paused to recover and replied confidently: *'Let's begin with the first'*.
He fended me off again: *'That was all so long ago'*.

I stared directly back at him.
Then he made a weary appeal: *'But we went over it so many times'*.

I continued staring. He was wrong. We didn't ever go over it.
Then he said: *'There's nothing I could have done differently anyway'*. This closed it down.

I felt crushed into the carpet, and my voice squeaky and trembling said: *'What about the second marriage?'*
He became flustered and his eyes twitched: *'I'd rather talk about the future'*. He was running away.

My eyes filled up, and a sob pushed up from the middle of my chest. As I'd always expected, Dad had no real interest in my feelings or needs. With shaking hands I topped up our cups and offered a ginger biscuit. After a couple of sips, I asked about his wedding plans, but my voice was still feeble. He answered, but I don't remember what he said because I wasn't interested.

Five minutes later he left, apparently untroubled, leaving me humiliated and shaking with rage. He'd also given me another masterclass in avoidance. He refused to reflect because he believed he was unable to change.

In 1990, after a further six years of dashed hopes and superficiality, Dad phoned me with a surprising request. He wanted what he called 'atonement', but he offered nothing in return: no apology, no contrition, no reflection, and no acknowledgement of the difficulties of his five sons. Had he not noticed their reluctance to visit, the unreturned calls, our cold shoulders,our flaring tempers, our refusals to hug and the ambivalence running through our forced chat? Perhaps he had, but he didn't say. Had he shown care or curiosity when our tempers flared? No, or if he had he didn't say. Did he pause to reflect when his downstairs windows were smashed by one son or when another made a suicide attempt? He just wanted the family to forgive him, without admitting his contribution to our difficulties. I told him it was too late.

This summarised Dad's comings and goings. Like the father he met in the psychodrama at the lighthouse, our Dad knew how to make his young boys howl, but we did so quietly.

He died ten years later in November 2000.

*

The taxi arrived and drove me for 45 minutes to Mauerbach, a small town in the hills to the northwest of Vienna. I was about to spend the afternoon with a team of senior leaders in charge of manufacturing for a large international company. There were Belgians, Austrians, Norwegians, Dutch and a Swede on the team, in total twelve people I'd not met before, ten men and two women.

Current low levels of production were causing serious frustrations amongst their sales colleagues who resented missing their bonus. Their overriding team objective was to increase the safety and reliability across dozens of production sites making it possible to ramp up production volumes. Through coaching and facilitation, I was to help improve the quality of their conversations, and build an agenda of priority discussion topics.

As I stepped out of the taxi, the sky was blue, the lawns were manicured and the site was surrounded by forested hills. Those similarities with my trip in the Fiat camper van to Germany in 1972, jumped out at me.

As the team assembled in the meeting room, I placed four labels on the floor (Warrior, Dreamer, Thinker and Lover, from an article in the McKinsey Quarterly) and told them all four roles are needed in any team. I invited everyone to stand beside the label that described their best contribution to the team.

Six of them moved immediately to the Warrior place, three to Thinker, Two to Dreamer and one to Lover.

I asked the Warriors why they needed the others. They told me they needed a Thinker to identify the risks, a Dreamer to raise new ideas and possibilities and a Lover to draw people into the work and improve the implementation. This lesson was to demonstrate why everyone's contribution was needed. In those discussions, the team members got to know one another better.

Next, I invited pairs to come up with one or two priority items for the agenda. Once we'd eliminated overlaps, this produced a nine-item agenda on the flipchart. They cast votes to agree where to start and we sat in a circle to discuss the first topic. When time ran out they summarised their conclusion. I asked them to reflect on the quality of this conversation: they said it was more honest and more disciplined than usual, without speaking in circles, and unusually they had reached a clear conclusion.

That afternoon was a step-up in this team's performance, leaving them with a specific outcome on the topic discussed, a new sense of confidence and a clear intention to continue practising the simple tools I had given them. Had this unlocked their potential as a team? Undoubtedly yes. And their potential as individuals? Yes to that too.

As I climbed into the taxi bound for the airport, the sky was still blue, the lawns manicured and framed by forested hills. The trip to Germany in 1972 was still running through my mind. We sped along the autobahn and I asked myself: could the Mauerbach session have accomplished all this if the Human Potential Movement had never happened? Probably not, because the methods I used with the team had all been created in the wake of that Movement.

I reflected on the notes I'd written about Dad earlier that morning, and summed up my parents' relationship like this: Dad was a Dreamer-Warrior and Mum by covering his weaknesses in the Thinker-People arena, protected the family. When they became polarised and typecast in those different roles, this destroyed their marriage.

# Part Five:
# Growing From Our Roots

## Chapter 22: Us

On the Thursday evening, after a busy afternoon with the client team at Mauerbach, I boarded the plane at Vienna International. Once in the air, my earphones blotted out the announcements. On the laptop, I completed my account of Dad's closing years interrupted that morning by the taxi's arrival.

*

A few months before Dad dies, we share a meaningful exchange I have long hoped for. A stroke has put him in a costly seaside care home. His basic needs are taken care of (food, shelter and warmth), but this is a "gilded cage" of overheated rooms, and the enticing expansive gardens are denied to him by the locked French windows. The sign-in book betrays that we are his first visitors for many weeks.

Helen borrows a wheelchair and we push him along uneven pavements, against a stiff breeze blowing up from the sea, to a fish and chip lunch in his favourite seaside pub. While Helen is queuing up for food, Dad grabs the moment and beats his difficulty forming words:
*She…'* he says
*'Yes?'* I reply.
*'She… probably… does not… re.. mem.. ber… who I am?'*
I make a guess at *'she'*: 'Do you mean Mum?'
*'Yes.'*

This is astonishing because Dad hasn't spoken of Mum since the mid 1970s.
*'Are you saying Mum doesn't remember you?'*
*'Yes.'*

I wonder, is Dad finally trying to answer my question, the one he always dodges about why he split up from Mum? I disagree with him: *'She will always remember you, despite her dementia, just as she still remembers me'.* It's what I choose to believe.

He continues: *'I thought she was too soft with you… and the other children'.*

When he says this, the inter-generational echo strikes me: Grandpa's harsh punishments were to drive out the softness he perceived in Dad as a child. When grown up and married, Dad expected Mum to continue Grandpa's battle against softness, by being stricter with us. Mum opposed Dad in this matter, and a rift opened up between them.

What Dad says next is remarkable too. He offers Mum's side of an old argument: *'She said I failed to take people's feelings into account, and she advised me always to choose the path that will be kinder for all concerned'.*
It's remarkable he managed to declare this, because Dad always had difficulty seeing another person's point of view.

Then he explains his own side: *'I wanted her to make you stronger, and for everyone to take more risks, I've wanted to tell you this, for a long time… but she does not like it when I talk to you'.*
With that, I am confused: *'She? Who is she? Who does not like you to talk to me?'*

In response, Dad gives me a sharp look and takes a moment to find the words: *'I mean my present wife. It disturbs her. She is afraid when we talk like this, that we will open a box, and never close it again.'*

I feel warmth when he says *'when we talk like this',* because he's saying what we're doing is special, between him and me.
With a smile, I reply: *'Luckily she doesn't know we are talking now!'* The visitor book has shown me that Dad's present wife (number three) is keeping her distance.

Dad gives me a crooked smile back. "Fun Dad" is making a fleeting return.

\*

That exchange happened before Helen returned with our fish and chips lunches. It was Dad's belated attempt to patch things up between us, and fell short of the repair I felt entitled to. But it was something.

*

I've often pondered a question: when did a distortion occur that bent me out of shape and produced this sixty-year-old haunted by his childhood? The original rupture occurred long ago as a boy growing up, perfectly normally, making friends and growing in independence.

It happened at thirteen, because before that Dad was devoted to helping other people. In the summer of 1968, he moved the family to Rochester, for him not for us. I lost my old friends, but I was thrilled to spend each day, just the two of us in each other's company doing the rewiring. When August ended, Dad dumped me for a new job that drew him inexorably into what I now call his "cult of self". You don't need to understand the Human Potential Movement to know that Dad was walking away and spoiling everything between us.

After 1968, he continued the pattern: a long period of absence, and he would return out of nowhere with a crazy event: at Bawdsey Estuary, then the "revelation", and yes, the next crazy event was the death of my sister, and I wanted to blame Dad for that too. Only with the trip to Germany, did it finally sink in: Dad was walking out of the family, and it was personal.

If our family was a fine porcelain vase, Dad was smashing it into tiny pieces. I kept picking up a handful of pieces but I couldn't ever satisfy my deep-felt need to reassemble them without Dad's help, and he wasn't offering this.

The last time I saw him, classical music was playing. The bedside photo showed him as a child playing with his sister and brother. They say the child is father to the man, but inevitably the man becomes a child again.

He was lying on his back, body shrivelled beneath the sheets, hands on top, eyes closed, and a rattly breath flowing in and out of an open O. I laid my hand on his, producing a flutter from his closed eyelids. Because the nurse said hearing is the last sense to go, I said this out loud: *'I was angry when you left and after that we kept missing each other'.* I was telling him the truth, giving him respect, and at the same time forgiving myself. He had stretched me and made me brave, but he left unfinished business.

His breathing sped up briefly, then it was over. I kissed his forehead and left the room, believing Dad had taken his secrets to the grave. It was a few weeks later when I first saw his secret box.

## Chapter 23: Wishful Thinking

I must have gone to sleep on the return flight from Vienna, because I awoke to the ping of the seatbelt lights. Dragging myself back into the present, I noticed this story of Dad was approaching a landing.

In the arrivals lounge at Heathrow, a driver was holding up my name on a board. That evening, I gave Helen my new perspectives from Vienna about Freud, Dad and Grandpa and the Human Potential Movement. As for the part about Germany, I said it would be interesting to go back, because Germany was where a penny once dropped.

If we returned, our trip would be different because it was not only about me, but also about Helen and me. We had been friends for forty-three years, lovers for forty years, married for thirty-six years, and parents for twenty-nine years. With our children planted out, we were entering the uncertainties of retirement.

I said why not give ourselves a little adventure? Why not make space for the questions that naturally arise at our stage of life? What do we still have time for? What new challenges do we want to take on? How do we want to live? How might we feel different and better when we return?

It was a relief when Helen agreed. We were nearing the end of June 2016, and a few weeks later we put our plan into action.

*

It is seven thirty on a sunny Thursday morning in August 2016, and our white Mini Cooper is setting out on the planned eight-hour, four hundred and fifty mile road trip. I am the more eager. Helen alternates between dozing and drinking coffee. When the caffeine kicks in witty observations and questions come out of her: *'Why are "Coming of Age" stories always about teenagers?'*

It is rhetorical. We are setting our minds free here, letting ourselves relax and depressurise. Of course the German Summer School was a "Coming of Age" bound up with the tricky business of growing up. After this I was furious about Dad's two-timing, and Dad was a God-in-ruins. Then the silence lasted for decades, until Dad's strokes and Mum's dementia, with much left unsaid and unfinished.

We drive onto the ferry for the two hour crossing to Dunkirk, and we sit in a crowded coffee lounge where kids are running around, immersed in conversation. We have enjoyed and survived a lifetime of births, marriages, divorces, deaths, and much more. We're at the end of parenting and working. I mention Shakespeare's Seven Ages of Man. We are beyond the warrior stage, but thankfully not yet at imminent death.

Helen says: *'Can we be like snakes, shedding a skin?'* It's a provocation to notice no one is exempt: like it or not, at sixty you're in a "Rite of Passage" that brings a "Separation" and a "Transition" before you can enter the next phase. She adds: *'How can we untangle ourselves from the past?'*

A loudspeaker beneath rusty paint crackles the order to return to our cars. With a metallic clunk, the ramp deposits our car and its contents in France. "Separation" is over, and we enter the "Transition": I'm driving on the right instead of the left, taking in the different road signs, and checking at roundabouts for cars shooting into our path. Soon we enter Belgium, with its slightly different speed limits. We settle down for the six-hour drive past Brussels to our hotel near Koblenz. We have a lot to talk about and plenty of time. The conversation drifts to and fro.

I ask: *'How can we separate the truth from the lies?'*
Helpfully Helen summarises what we know about my family of origin:
*'In the end it's a lot more to do with your Dad than your sister isn't it?'*

The big question, after eighteen months on the quest, is can we overturn two lies, a "harmless lie" that my sister died of a cancer I didn't recognise, and a "convenient lie" that my sister's death was to blame for my parents' divorce?

The copy we requested of my sister's death certificate has recently arrived in the post. The "First Cause" given for her death is *'Ovarian Cancer'*. Damn! Exactly as Auntie M said, and the "Final Cause" is given as *'Carcinomatosis Via Lymph Nodes'* which I've checked means a spread of cancer through the body. There's no mention of blood cancer, which was the second opinion my parents told me was the truth. We're left to conclude that blood cancer was just a next stage as the ovarian cancer was spreading. Perhaps my parents were too deep in grief to explain, but what I've since labelled the "harmless lie" wasn't a lie at all.

Helen brings us to "convenient lie" which is our real point: *'A cancer was spreading in your parents' marriage long before your sister died. Her death can't be the "First Cause", of their break up, but we can't rule it out as the "Final Cause"'*.

For both our benefits, I run through a pile of possible "First Causes": Grandpa's interference, the humpback bridge, Granny moving in, Dad's falling into religion and politics, his missions and great ambitions, his dodgy colleagues, the Human Potential Movement, his madness at the Estuary and the "revelation", his infidelity with Eve and Cal, and many more. I don't even go into Dad's upbringing or how Grandpa was affected by the wars.

As for the "Final Cause", I still can't swallow that my sister's death in September 1971 did it for the marriage. We can show that her illness reunited my parents when they had been at loggerheads, and surely this increased their chances of a reconciliation?

After Brussels, the aircon is blasting. We turn it off and open the windows as we head towards Aachen and the German border, but it's too hot and the wind battering our ears makes it impossible to talk. We close the windows again, and try to pin down what was really going on with Dad, to help us get to the "Final Cause".

Helen dives straight in: *'He was a Jekyll and Hyde, pretending to be good like Dr Jekyll, but the Human Potential Movement was his drug, making him as bad as Mr Hyde'*.
I throw another story back: *'Or Walter Mitty, an ordinary man telling unbelievable stories about being extraordinary'*.

We replay some recollections from my cousins. Cousin K remembers Dad's erratic driving. Cousin C liked Dad for being different and not terribly straightforward. Cousin W remembers days out when Dad encouraged her to tightrope walk along logs, and high walls, never to be afraid of falling off. Dad wanted everyone to have the courage to take risks.

The risk-taking evidence was there at the Humpback Bridge, the Estuary and in the "revelation", and this brought a new insight: each time Dad took a risk, he placed a bet on his own success. He bargained with God. He convinced himself all would be fine. He believed in the power of positivity. This was Dad's wishful thinking. Two books on his shelf encouraged this approach: "The Will To Believe" by William James (passed on by Grandpa) and "The Power of Positive Thinking" by Normal Vincent Peale (an American priest who was influenced by various psychiatrists). Dad came to believe in belief itself.

Wishful thinking pervaded our young lives. While Uncle J was a scientist interested in facts, by contrast Dad was an unscientific scientist who clung to belief. Mum was different again: she was a sceptic, regarding both those men as grandiose and foolish. Shortly before her hysterectomy in the summer term of 1966, we were driving to my interview at Maidstone Grammar School. Dad wanted to cheer Mum up by asking about Mum's dreams for the future. She said: *'I dream for our children to do really well in their exams, and for us one day to have a family reunion in California'.* We both listened carefully to that. We wanted Mum to get better, and to believe her dreams could happen, as in a sense they almost did.

Dad wanted to prove the power of dreams, and I could have easily been convinced, until the three hammer blows (the move to Rochester, the Estuary and the "revelation") made me sceptical, more like Mum. If you believe in belief, wishful thinking can grip you. If you are like Dad, the doors then close behind you, and there is no practical way out. You will concoct bets, bargains and beliefs. You will pray. You will stop seeing reality. You will rejoice at the evidence that confirms what you want to believe, and discard the rest. When you fall prey to this "confirmation bias", your feet will leave the ground.

Dad and Mum argued about this. In the midst of my sister's illness, Dad was eager to use the power of prayer, while Mum relied on the medicine.

We enter Germany where two autobahns merge and the road jams up. The heat hits us when we step out onto melting tarmac to swap drivers. We shut the doors quickly and continue the story under the aircon, while we wait for the traffic to move.

I tell Helen what I've found out about Dad's "big decision". The timing was no coincidence either. On the 27th July 1971, in the midst of my sister's illness, Mum wrote to Dad playing back his decision to change. The tone in her letter was cautious: she was writing down Dad's decision because Dad needed to be reminded he had promised to set himself new *'personal boundaries'* by ruling out extra-marital relationships and to resign at work. I say: *'Dad's like Hercules, strapping himself to the mast, resisting the beautiful sirens who want to drown him in deadly whirlpools'.*

It looked like Dad was making a bargain with God: giving up the freedom in return for his daughter's life. The tone of Dad's diary entries during July and half of August fitted this explanation: his daughter was to have an operation, *'everyone'* was confident about the surgery, optimism about the prospects for her recovery, when she came round *'everything'* had been a great success, *'big rejoicing'* when she came home. They made plans to go on a little holiday together. But reality quickly intruded: further hospital appointments, the second opinion, re-admission, blood transfusions, chemo and radiotherapy. By mid-August Dad's optimism had disappeared, and his diary entries ceased altogether.

In September 1971, following their daughter's death, Mum and Dad deep in grief, descended into blame and recrimination. Dad complained of Mum's failure to support his campaign of faith and prayer, while she complained of his failure to secure the correct medical treatment. It only got worse and the rest of the family knew more than we did. Cousin V in Yorkshire said it all boiled down to sex, and that Mum said: *'That's it, no more sex, I no longer have the appetite'.* Dad replied: *'Then I'll find another woman who does, one who can give me another child'.*

With this, Dad's "big decision" was revoked: God had failed to save the daughter, so Dad was no longer required to keep his side of the bargain. He embarked on a deliberate search for a new partner and, instead of resigning, he continued with the firm.

We're heading towards Cologne. Helen is driving, and we're assembling the jigsaw. Helen returns to our archetypal stories: *'So he's diving back into those deadly whirlpools'*.
I try another: *'Maybe like Icarus, whose father gave him wax wings that melt when he flies too close to the sun?'*

It's thirty-four degrees centigrade. We're hungry and, with delays ahead, we divert into a small town hoping for a bratwurst. We can only find coffee and ice-cream, but that is OK. We continue on small roads. After Bonn, we follow the west bank of the Rhine, and Helen is thoughtful, then suddenly we're laughing because she remembers Dad's "rebirthing": *'Are you serious he tried to wipe his memory?'*
I nod. He wanted a fresh start.

Helen asks: *'Would that be a fresh start with his old or his new family?'* It was a pertinent question. She adds: *'And how well did it work?'*
I didn't need to answer: we'd gone over the details already. Dad felt tricked by the rebirthing, because afterwards he was just as torn between the past and the present. Mum agreed to a reconciliation in December 1974 and the marriage resumed, but on Dad's triangular terms, with him hopping between. The man threw everyone into confusion with his lies, constant zig-zagging and wishful thinking.

Helen said: *'He's still Pinocchio then, the lazy puppet who can't help telling lies'.*

Dad was lying to keep his triangle in place, against the wishes of Mum, Shirley and all the children who were suffering complex and uncomfortable feelings due to being in competition.

At last we are pinning down the "Final Cause" of their break up, and it's a bit of a surprise when we work out it was Mum. Mum's letter to Dad in which she was re-arranging the furniture (covered earlier) marked the ending. She wrote it after her decision to reinstate the divorce proceedings.

Dad left Mum a final present: a slim Penguin paperback with a plain black cover, called "Knots" by the rebirthing psychiatrist R D Laing. When Mum died, it was passed on to me. My hands tremble and my chest flutters when I hold it, and I feel sad all over again, because of Dad's inscription inside the front cover:

*'To N,*
*In penitence and love,*
*D*
*(No acknowledgement, please)'.*

The last line in brackets still catches me unawares. It makes no sense.

Helen pulls me back: *'So can we say Dad was the "First Cause" of the marriage breakdown, and Mum, by resuming divorce proceedings, was the "Final Cause"'.*

I am satisfied with that and we move into the here and now: *'Unlike Dad, we know where we are driving to and why'.* Light-heartedly, Helen builds on this: *'My English teacher said our stories are like a bus ride to Leeds. We have to know two things: why we are compelled to get on the bus, and what terrible thing will befall us if we don't'.*

In reply I joke that my wife has demons and sulks unless I travel with her.
Helen jokes back: *'No. It's this. A husband retires and secretly expects to live the dream. But his wife clings to the familiar. So he launches them into a wild foreign adventure!'*

I say: *'OK let's make this trip a wild one!'*

But after a day on the autobahn in scorching heat we're not up for anything wild. We are arriving tired at our hotel in Neuwied, a village north of Koblenz. The hotel is a beautifully restored factory-owner's house. It's baking inside and a big family party has taken over the restaurant. We're happy to go out for pizza and beer in the village square.

When we get back, we open the bedroom window for a breeze and try to get some sleep, because there's a big day ahead.

# Chapter 24: Coming Back To Life

The next morning, we follow the east bank of the Rhine southwards with the river on our right, until Marksburg Castle looms over us, and the road winds upwards through overhanging trees rooted in the Taunus mountainside. We emerge into sunlight on the top of the world, where the road sign *'Adolphus Busch Alle',* the kerbs and high railings look suburban amidst undulating farmlands stretching to a forested horizon.

Also oddly in this rural scene, laughing young men in green overalls are engaged in pushing a laundry trolley up the gentle incline, and riding down it again.

We park. It is 10am and the air is already warming up. We walk in through tall iron gates and I suppress a wave of nostalgia. A signpost in a neatly clipped azalea hedge points us to Villa Lilly. We pass more staff in green overalls, sweeping the paths and weeding the flowerbeds. A young blond woman is clipping a hedge, beside a washing line of baby clothes. We come to a turreted house, with crested roof, orange bricks and grey timbered conservatory. It is familiar from long ago.

Steep steps and a stained glass front door bring us into Villa Lilly. A noticeboard in the hall announces our visit as today's event. Good, we're expected. We take seats outside an office door. A young man in green, with beads of sweat on his nose, rushes past us and pushes open the office door: *'Entschuldigung. Ein Moment bitte'.* Refused entry, he retreats and paces nervously in front of us. Then it clicks: he is a patient, because Villa Lilly is now a centre for the rehabilitation of crystal-meth addicts. We're sitting outside a therapist's room.

When the door opens again, the addict looks up expectantly, but we are summoned in. A staff member redirects us from *'Villa Lilly Haus'* to *'Villa Lilly Dorf'*, a five minute walk cross the grounds. We arrive at a portakabin beside a bed of roses, containing the office of Johann Muller, Therapy Manager. He appears in a yellow polo shirt, denim trousers with un-socked feet in brown leather sandals, greeting us in English with hand outstretched, and offering coffee.

His office is bright, a wall lined with books and a cluttered desk. Johann fishes out a DVD and a colourful children's story set in the grounds of Villa Lilly. He summarises his thirty years of drug therapy at this place, and adds in some history too. These are already great gifts, more than justifying our long drive.

The therapy is fascinating. Each year, 250 patients complete a ten-month programme, making a tally of 7000 patients over the thirty years of operation. After their first four months here, each patient is challenged to spend a day in a neighbouring town, with a drug test on their return. A tiny trace of drugs or alcohol will trigger instant expulsion, and the patients themselves insist on this strictness. The treatment achieves an impressive fifty percent success rate.

When ex-patients return for the annual reunion, Johann remembers most of them still. Last time a young woman said *'Hello I'm Nina'*, but Johann was blank until the patient added *'And of course this is my mother Sylvie'*. Johann knew Sylvie, but not her daughter Nina, who was only four when the treatment was completed.

In response to our questions about the therapy, Johann points out the patients' artwork on his wall. Above Helen's head is a framed print showing two plates of pasta, one jumbled up represented *'me when I came in'*, and the other with pasta neatly in lines was *'me now'*.

A huge canvas dominates the other wall. Rough brushstrokes depict a person in a lush dark forest, his head luminous in bright green, and his body consumed by bright red flames. Johann explains: *'This self-portrait was left by a patient pleading: "Please keep it displayed always". He's a professional artist now in Berlin and still clean'*.

As for the history, Villa Lilly was built by Adolphus Busch, a brewer, who married Lilly Anheuser, the daughter of a brewer from St Louis Missouri in 1861. They became the owners of Budweiser, the biggest beer company in the world and returned each summer to what was known locally as The Beer King's Castle. Later it became a school, then a base for the Nazis and, after the allied victory, for the American troops. They remember that Rita Heyworth danced here with the Americans. After the German state of Hesse purchased the estate from the Anheuser-Busch family in 1961, the houses were renovated and the estate was rented to a German satirical magazine (something like Private Eye), and later to a community of Timothy Leary inspired LSD-users.

When Michael asks about my previous visit, I tell him about the 1972 summer school put on for the Human Potential Movement, to release the untapped potential of those who came, in furtherance of their belief that by growing themselves they would improve society. Michael nodded and seemed to go along with that belief, then asked how the event was organised.

I replied: *'Dad's membership of Association of Humanistic Psychology (AHP) allowed him to send out the invitations through AHP branches across Europe, bringing in the British, French, Belgian, Dutch, Swiss, Germans and Americans who attended'.*

Ironies leap out of our stories: a drug and alcohol free zone built by the world's biggest alcohol salesman? A treatment centre for crystal-meth and cocaine addictions, after the Nazis once based here were infamous for using such drugs without restraint? Dad's summer school encouraging US government sponsored human growth as an antidote to totalitarian rule, then an LSD-sect run by Otto Muehl, who was a former Nazi officer and autocratic cult leader sentenced in 1991 for sex crimes and drugs offences?

When we remark on those ironies, Johann sucks in and bares his teeth: *'Don't be cynical. This is a special place'*. He tells us irony is destructive because it corrodes our beliefs, and beliefs matter hugely. Adolphus Busch **believed** Villa Lilly was a special place. When he died his body was buried in America, but his heart had to be cut out and buried here in a special burial place in the woods. The success of Johann's treatment regime depends on belief, and cynicism causes relapse.

When we shake hands to leave, Johann's eye contact is direct and he extends an invitation: *'Walk anywhere you like in the Villa Lilly estate, but please don't talk to the patients'*. We re-trace my steps from long ago, going to the terrace where Dad was so happy and animated during the first summer school breakfast. We stroll through sun-dappled, overgrown orchards where I wandered with my brother bored, towards the place where I sunbathed and the naked people appeared. Today's weather is just as sunny. We photograph the *"Menschen Verboten"* sign on the dumbwaiter in which my brother and I took illicit rides. We rediscover the schoolhouse we burgled and the room in the art nouveau house where we sheltered under thunder and lightning. We find the cosy room where, after that storm, in front of a warm fire, I first felt like an adult.

I am blissfully happy wandering again in these grounds. Helen is remarkably patient, until just before midday I say: *'OK, that's enough'.*

We get back into the car and, as we drive down the mountain towards the Rhine below, we are bathed in sunlight and gentle positivity. This dreamy feeling carries us through the afternoon. While driving, Helen reminds us of another enchanted house: *'Your Mum and Auntie G curled up my hair using a sugar solution, and I wore your Mum's gold brocade dress. It was the last grand garden party for that bungalow in Kent, before its demolition. Remember the glowworms. How luminous and magical!'*

She asks: *'But what is a glowworm actually?'*
I improvise: *'Unlike worms that burrow in the dark underground, their cousin the glowworm flies and shines a light'.*
Laughing, she catches me: *'You don't even know! And you're leaving out the feeling. To see a glowworm is beautiful like the Northern Lights coming out of the night sky. You can't help but go wow!'*
We are light-hearted and playful with words: *'Low becomes glow, loss becomes gloss'.*
*'Litter becomes glitter, listen becomes glisten...'*
*'... and lad becomes glad'.*

We flit here and there, without needing to explain. Our advancing hunger gets woven in: *'We're free to choose...from the food that runs through our bodies...'*
*'... to the quality that runs through our lives.'*
We're glowing ourselves by now. We don't need to say it, but we

are talking about love, which eases the most difficult things, like stepping back to let our children grow up, like retiring from work, and moving forward into a new phase in our lives.

We sit down on the riverbank for a picnic of bread and cheese, watching nimble tourist cruisers vie with lumbering great cargo barges. This river, which has inspired great poets as it gouges its path between steep banks, is lined with the ancient castles of traders and producers of fine wines. Romantic Rhine Gorge is a fluid border separating people of the East and West, and also connecting them.

After lunch, a small ferry carries us across fast-flowing water to the west bank. In sweltering heat, we walk through the town of Boppard. Then rising on a chairlift into an infinity of cooler air, our horizons expand. Below us, we see the river, road and railway snaking through empty vineyards and quiet hamlets towards more cluttered worlds. The beauty and immensity are over-whelming, until the chairlift judders to a halt, and instantaneously our world shrinks. We dangle in our little chair from the flimsy wire, terrified. We doubt we can survive the thirty-metre drop to a rocky floor. We try to focus on specifics: the train snaking round the mountain. We search for a favourite tree. But it's impossible to escape the terror that has invaded us. After an age, the lift resumes. We disembark high on the mountain, carrying with us that vivid new lesson in fear.

A cool walk through woods brings us to a café at the peak, and I gaze in calm equanimity across the river towards the Taunus Mountains where, in 1972, my adult life began. I register that over the years work has too often consumed me, like the flaming man on Johann's office. I brought this obsession to the quest, and now it is time to let it go.

Resting in the cool above the Rhine Gorge, Helen turns serious too: *'I used to believe, with Hitler toppled, peace would reign for ever'*.
*'And children used to believe in magic'*, then I tick myself off for this cynicism.
Helen's face drops: *'But the world goes backwards too. There are food banks. Brexit. Terrorists on the streets. New baddies popping up. All kinds of madness'*.

Suddenly up there on the hill, our lives seem fragile and incendiary. Just like the flaming addict, we can become interested only in ourselves. Just like the addict, we can be saved by another's belief in us, and in our capacity, despite the evident risks, to withstand the difficulties of being alive. With drugs burning up his body, he was saved by Johann's belief in him and his capacity to withstand the difficulties of being alive. With this, the patient ventured out on a new path, leaving the flaming addict behind.

But how to stay clean? Through a kind of belief. The addict is strengthened through the belief that Johann the therapist is still watching him, and in turn the therapist is strengthened by his belief in the specialness of a place called Villa Lilly where history moves through cycles, inexorably out of the despair even when the odds are stacked against us, restoring us to hope.

We remember the secret Johann told us that morning: *'It's in their eyes. You know the patient's clean when you can finally see them properly. Of course people fall over, but the real question is, can they get themselves up again. If they have learned to get up here, then they have hope'.*

We remember the moment  we shook hands with Johann to say goodbye. He locked eyes with us. I felt his eyes checking me, certifying me clean, then I felt free.

With the day's thoughts still swirling round our heads, Helen and I take the chair lift down, and this time our mood is relaxed: we hardly notice the drop. We are buoyed up with confidence about new possibilities awaiting us.

The following day renewed confidence accompanies us north, and back to our life.

*

A few days after arriving home, I still felt a glow. It had taken over 40 years to complete a circle. Villa Lilly was the closest Dad came to creating a "mini-society", and it lasted just three weeks, but it was a pivotal moment for him and me. His relaxed face at breakfast the first morning betrayed the significance to him:

his life had taken a turn. Now I know, that at the summer school Dad was preparing himself to dive into a new family, despite his misgivings about separating from us. Dad's refusal to explain himself, and my refusal to accept his decision to depart, made it impossible to bring the old and new parts of Dad's life together into peaceful co-existence.

Dad's final visit to our home in London was in a wheelchair after his first stroke, five years before he died, and before he went into a home. We were giving his third wife a break from him. Dad wanted to make himself useful, so we gave him a small patch of wallpaper to scrape off in the room we were decorating. I made myself helpful too, listening while haltingly Dad told me about the hypnotherapy training in which his grandfather was the topic, because Dad believed that man's monstrous anger was the source of our family's trouble. Later that day when Dad needed a bath, I was lifting him in and I couldn't help looking at the little willy which contributed greatly to our family troubles.

I said to myself: *'if only Dad could have reflected on his parenting…',* but then he once did. On my visit to Kenya in 1973, he told me his latest pet theory: *'Strict and Critical Parents produce a Conformist or Rebellious Child'.* Now I can see he was both of those children and his mid-life rebellion was against his parents' over-bearing control. But back then I realised with disappointment that he wasn't reflecting on his years as my parent, he was talking about his parenting tactics for the new family. Oddly, I also felt pleased to have him addressing me as an adult: the grown up Sunny Jim.

Inspired by our recent "rite of passage" in Germany, I summarised for one last time the story I wanted to put to rest:

*No one's perfect.*

*When his birth father walked away, a son became an orphan, lost and ashamed. The dad was obsessed with something, and the son became obsessed with finding out what. The son's questions were met with silence. When the son grew up he tried to repair things with the dad, but this only produced a superficial friendship, until the dad died.*

*The dad left behind a box of secrets, and after fifteen more years the son finally opened the box to find a muddle of papers that he took to be a warning: don't leave a muddle behind for your children: give them the story they deserve. And more importantly, don't turn into your dad.*

*Long and painstaking work on that muddle revealed this story of dad. A man's childhood was blighted by an absent father who tried to save the world. A woman's childhood was blighted by her mother's inability to hold onto her father. That man and woman were happily married, and agreed to raise their children without ever speaking of the past. The fun-seeking and generous young dad took on increasing responsibility (with job, wife, home, kids, and outside activities including sport, church, politics, not to mention other women). He was eager to please, but under the load he became stressed and thoughtless. The mum accused him of a callous disregard for others, but refused to let the dad drift away. The dad changed nothing and continued dragging his burden.*

*Despite burying the horrors of their past, their present lives were turning nasty. The Human Potential Movement promised the dad a magical liberation. He became drawn in, as if to a cult, which baffled his family who felt all the more ignored and neglected. And the dad, baffled by their bafflement, could not explain himself.*

*The son, when he discovered the dad's story, experienced a new clarity: his parents loved him and made a happy home, eager to erase their own crippling childhoods, while the past still haunted them. No one tried harder than the dad to save the world or the mum to hold onto the dad, but to no avail. Dad had turned into his father, and Mum into her mother.*

*The son was left with a permanent mark from the break up: a legacy. He was in no danger of turning into his dad because he discovered a different passion: to dig out and tell untold stories, stories of hopeful realism that made sense to a mum who was realistic, and to a father who was hopeful. His stories avoided the pitfalls of despair and the pipe dreams of delusion, they fostered respect and appreciation, enlarging our understanding of those who depend on us, by including their different points of view.*

This story lightened my heart, and washed away the last traces of negativity surrounding the momentous events of my childhood. This completed the exorcism because I no longer felt troubled, and I could find no more shred of sourness in me. It raised the thorny question of forgiveness: did I forgive Dad?

But what kind of son presumes the right to forgive his parents? I can say for sure I am not that kind of a son. My parents did their best. I accept them and it is not for me to forgive them. The tension has departed, and I am no longer confused.

I spotted a book on a shelf at Villa Lilly called "The Prophet". We also had a copy but when we got back home I couldn't find it. I searched for quotes from the book using the Internet, and I enjoyed once again its wisdom about life, family, friendship, children, parents, home, pleasure and loss. As I read these, I became overtaken by a feeling I couldn't name: a nostalgia with a tinge of optimism, and an urge to act. I ordered two copies, and sent them to my two brothers with a bridge-building note, which tried to say: *'No one did anything wrong'*.

## Chapter 25: Closing The Box

It is November 2016, and I awake with a jolt of surprise to find I am in a room by the beach at Hua Hin. Each morning we do pre-breakfast yoga on the sand while the sun, peeping through passing clouds, rises higher over the sea. It is warm enough not to be bothered by the tail-end of the monsoon.

We check out the local sights: a rocky headland with a Buddhist temple, and the ornate royal pavilion converted into a stunning railway station. Marigold-strewn street shrines play jazz music through little speakers, in homage to the saxophone-playing king just deceased. Dark clothes are being worn, out of respect for a ruler who was like a father.

Father? For twenty-eight years from his moving out until his death, our "friendship" consisted of superficial meetings and missed opportunities. I longed for a closeness, while refusing to turn into his kind of Dad.

At these Thailand shrines, Glenn Miller's "In The Mood" sets me off and I choke to suppress sobs. I hold onto Helen and say goodbye again to a needy, narcissist, idealist Don Quixote of a Dad, in all four versions. Goodbye to the one who winks at me after the humpback bridge, but I vow to hold onto his spontaneous fun. Farewell to the strict one who works selflessly and tirelessly, but I hold onto his generosity. Ta-ra to the one who believes he is chosen to create the "mini-society" and denies the mayhem and hurt he causes to his family, but I hold onto his courage to challenge the status quo. Finally goodbye to the one who starts anew but can't leave himself behind, and I hold onto his touching faith in human potential. I stand in awe of the capabilities this man sensed in each of us, but remember with dismay his efforts at taking this forward.

My long slow blink gives a moment for those four ghostly Dads to fade, and I re-open my eyes to the prospect of a lighter, more spontaneous me. A new chapter is starting for us, after the thrill of a quest that brought me through curiosity and confusion into anger, and the ritual journey that brought us to Germany and back.

In Hua Hin, on a Thailand beach, we are in the "here and now", toes in the sand, paddling our feet. We are watching people fish and horses canter. We chat and laugh as we drift through beach bars and restaurants.  We are choosing who to be. We choose to be active. We do the yoga together. Helen teaches me Tai Chi. I run along beaches. We are creative too: Helen paints and I write stories. We give our time as volunteers, to become part of something, beyond our work and our children.

Then we're travelling to Bangkok where I'm running a workshop and Helen has to fly home. In the introduction, I show a picture of four stick-people in a line, with Helen and me on the outside with the two children, taller than us in the middle. I tell them we are empty-nesters, freeing ourselves up, doing Tai Chi, volunteering sometimes, working as much or little as we want. I am here to serve them in the meeting, but I will need their help, because a crisis prevented my co-facilitator from coming.

I ask everyone to stand up and find a space. We pat down our arms and legs, and rub our tummies. We take deep breaths. We swing our arms. We twist our wrists and pull some free, fresh energy into our chests. We let it tingle inside. Then we bend our legs and from half-squatting rise up, and throw forward our hands to rid ourselves symbolically of the toxic gloop we no longer need. Finally we stand, as if on a cloud, gently swaying from left to right. Everyone loves this Tai Chi that Helen taught me on Hua Hin beach. We move on to address the real challenges faced by this international NGO whose mission is to eradicate poverty. The workshop goes well, because the job is accomplished together.

As I get on the plane bound for home, our new chapter has begun. I am tired and expecting a satisfying sleep, so I don't expect a nightmare. I see Helen beside the Rhine, complaining the world is going backwards. Heart-wrenching scenes flash by. Innocent families are fleeing sectarian wars in the Middle East. Religions in conflict. Shootings on a Tunisian beach. Truck attacks in London, Boston, Paris and Nice. Everyone on high alert. The Occupy movement protests against the privilege of the one percents, while families depend on food banks. Robots replace jobs. Google dodges taxes. Twitter triggers storms. Facebook fuels depression. We're losing our children to this.

No one can stop the icecaps melting and plastic clogging the oceans. Random, chaotic and catastrophic events: Brexit. The US election. Fake news. Rigging. Hacking. Ransom demands. People powerless and aggressive. Race riots. Everyday sexism and abuse. Every issue becomes viral and inflammatory. Social unrest. The police engulfed. Fear turns us into animals.

The nightmare only lasts a few minutes, mashing together the gloomiest stories in the world. The bad world dystopia is scarily real, bringing a crisis of passivity because the problems are so overwhelming.

Sleep is a long way off, so I pick up my book "The Death of Psychology" for something to read. Reasons for the nightmare start flooding my mind. I write them on my pad.

*The upheavals of the Industrial Revolution in the eighteenth and nineteenth centuries ripped apart families and communities across Europe. Spreading of science brought secularity, scepticism and rationalism, contributing to a loss of faith and the loosening of morality. The forces unleashed were simply too powerful for individuals to withstand. Psychic disturbance was showing as fear, depression, hysteria and aggression. Human madness was always expressed in brutality, amidst domestic, tribal and religious conflict.*

*Dictators were coming to power in the twentieth century, sparking bloody wars, at home and abroad. Psychology arrived with psychoanalysis (Freud and others) bringing to a tiny minority of people "solutions for the self" that were hardly scientific, while the wars butchered and traumatised the rest on an industrial scale.*

*The behaviourists (Watson, Skinner…) who came next claimed to be scientific, and failed to provide the deeper human insights people craved.*

This was turning into a rant, but I felt compelled to continue.

*The Second World War scattered my family across continents: Europe, Africa, America and Australia. They took themselves away into the vast fresh unknown, while at home, shattered societies were being rebuilt from the ashes of self-interest, fear and tribalism.*

*Psychologists got to work identifying the causes of war, researching authoritarianism (Zimbardo), conformity (Asch) and obedience (Milgram) while the US Military funded research to defend the nation against fascism and communism. The Human Potential Movement (HPM) sprang out of these post war efforts notably at NTL and Esalen, and created a new global appetite in people, to grow and develop themselves.*

*An anti-authoritarian climate flooded society in the late Sixties, bringing an individualism that made altruism passé and a cause for suspicion, nibbling away at the collective trust upon which the western establishment depended. This fuelled a "Cult of Self".*

With these panicky reflections, I am not simply sleepless, my stomach is churning. I'm sick and depressed. I'm not criticising my psychologist colleagues, but simply asking why do we fail to join the dots? Why don't we scale up our access and impact? How can people find the strength to lift themselves out of this chaos?

Finally, for calm, I embark on a different kind of story:

*We are billions of people, who as children believed there was only one story written down in a history book. But there was never one story. As we grew up we battled to impose our own stories, and we killed where necessary to prevail. We became sick of living and dying like that. One day we became curious, and counted up the stories properly. There were at least as many stories as people alive. None of these billions of stories was a clear winner, so humanity adopted a different approach. We began listening, with curiosity, to let ourselves be influenced by each and every story. As we continued to do so, our stories were joining up into one expansive story that embraced us all.*

Fanciful perhaps, but it works. I want to put this story in the gingham jar in the garden, to tell the aliens about our life on earth. And finally I fall asleep.

The landing at Heathrow is in the morning darkness. The cold

November air hits me hard after the soft humid heat of Thailand. I shiver on the bus coming home.

*

Helen opened the door to me and said: *'Do you remember the moon landing, when the astronauts took a giant leap for mankind?'* She was lost in her dreams.

I started jabbering about my bad world nightmare, the social upheavals and the puny efforts of psychologists, and this "now" world where everything is consumed thoughtlessly, and our "tit for tat" world with leaders who ignore their impacts and consequences.

Helen continued on her happy track: *'We had the first shots of the whole earth from outer space'.*
And I continued on mine: *'Yes but… today's world is full people erupting like me.'*

It bounced between us for a while: *'And we are the first generation with an Internet to reach across the entire planet instantaneously, to everyone'.*
*'Yes but… Facebook is just billions of people pumping themselves up and deflating others, spreading fake news, derailing elections, and promoting the nutters. This narcissism is an epidemic engulfing us, despite psychology, or possibly because of it.'*

We were planets colliding. Helen poetic and dreamy from sleep was softening my brittle edges and during a breakfast of fruit and toast, something different began to happen.
Helen said: *'At least social media shows everyone the bigger "us"'.*
I said: *'That feels about as fanciful as this..'*, and gave her my calming story from the plane: *'We are billions of people with six billion stories learning how to make one huge story that belongs to us all'.*

She smiled: *'It's when we chat, or sing songs. It's yoga classes and Tai Chi, it's what happens with dancing… and sex. Everyone is trying to fit their stories together'.*
I must have been too tired to keep up the angst and my heart

melted. We stood up and hugged. Gentler questions came to mind. The children. How did we make such beautiful people? How shall we use the time we have left? And how will we bow out gracefully?

I went upstairs for a catch-up sleep, and on the way stuck my head into the kids' bedrooms, empty of course. I spotted "The Prophet" on my son's bookshelf: the copy I'd mislaid, a gift from Mum at the time of his birth. As far as I knew, this was Mum's last compos mentis act. I searched through the book for a gem: *'Say not, "I have found the truth," but rather, "I have found a truth". For the soul unfolds itself, like a lotus of countless petals'.*

Truth. I paused to take it in. Mum said hold your truth lightly, share your things, take turns and, when you do that life will unfold nicely. I heard Mum's voice speak softly against the gentle rise and fall of her piano playing: Debussy's Arabesque.

Then I searched again for the advice to parents: *'Your children are not your children. They come through you but not from you. Their souls dwell in the house of tomorrow which you cannot visit, not even in your dreams'.*

Did this let parents let off the hook? Not entirely. Step away too soon, as Dad did, then the child remains entangled, as I was, and the parent might never be released.

Once in bed I slept easily.

*

Mum appears in my dream, her bouncy golden curls fading into grey, complaining bitterly about twenty wasted years.
I say: *'Nothing was for nothing. There was not one wasted day'.*
Then I add: *'But if Dad was kinder…'.*
Mum says: *'… he could have stayed. Thank you'.*

I ask: *'Thanks what for?'*
Mum replies: *'For refusing the "mini-society"'.*
I say: *'Dad was making such a mess'.*
She says: *'I'm sorry for leaving you with the mess'.*

Then I say: *'We each cleared it up, in our own way'.*
Mum smiles and says: *'Thanks for keeping an eye on the boys'.*
I flinch, and Mum's image fades.

*

On waking up, the mess of life still wasn't cleared away and the quest, which was all about my loyalty to my sister and to Dad, appeared much more to do with my loyalty to Mum.

*

It is midday. I am in the warmth of our house, feeling mellow and refreshed, standing with Helen looking out at the flowerbed where my spade unearthed the time capsule. That was eighteen months ago in May, when my known world was crumbling into the void of retirement.

Today, in November, the garden looks less cheerful but, inside my skin, belief in life is renewed, and I'm optimistic towards the children. We've been released by "The Prophet": when children grow up, it's no longer up to their parents to save them.

Next time our children see the black box it will be painted brightly, in yellows, oranges, reds and greens. The old diaries and letters will be gone. They'll find this manuscript, our snapshot of the flaming man at Villa Lilly, Grandpa's medals, and a carrot cake recipe handed down by Mum.

I'll say: *'This box is the legacy we're passing on to you. It's a store of inspiration for when you've fallen over, to lift you out of the chaos'.* I'll invite them to add their own mementos, because from the moment we hand it over it's their box not mine. I'll just add one tiny piece of advice:

*'Don't make it a box of secrets, as people did in the old days, because untold stories are poisonous, and as soon as a story is told, the healing begins'.*

# Appendix
# Reflections for Psychologists and the Helping Professions

As a son of the silent generation, somehow I arrived at a personal belief in the sheer good sense of writing and telling and passing on our stories, rather than burying the truths about our lives or erasing the memories. I hoped this insight and my means of arriving at it would be recognisable and even entertaining, but writing the story brought me to a professional question: *'so what?'* What about the professional implications I wondered, for practising psychologists, because I was one of those too, and what might this mean for the much larger community of those, perhaps not called psychologists, trusted to help other people with the challenges they face in that tricky business of being alive.

This appendix seeks to discuss the "so what", specifically in our relations with those others we seek to influence and help, when like goldfishes we can hardly see the water we're swimming in. If, as many of us suspect, we're being drawn in a "cult of self" then let's find some healthy ways out.

We begin with how I arrived as a psychologist (Appendix 1) with a belief in the value of story (Appendix 2), and continue with an attempt to weave together the story of our "cult of self" (Appendix 3). In the fourth appendix, we consider whether and how we can release ourselves from the stories that shaped us. Finally in Appendix 5 we reach towards some principles for finding a good place to stand in the human systems we inhabit and influence.

I offer this additional material with respect and humility towards colleagues, many of whom have more academic or practical knowledge than me.

# 1. On Becoming a Psychologist

I was a boy who followed his father into psychology and organisation development. Late in the 1980s, at the age of 32, I left a large management consultancy to become a self-employed Organisational Development Consultant, and it made sense to update my professional qualifications. With a good honours degree and ten years practical experience, I was eligible to join the British Psychological Society. I contacted an old professor to sign the forms. He advised me to keep reflecting on my experience and, where possible to write articles and share the learning more widely. I took his advice and, several months later I was let in, as an Associate Fellow.

I felt like a rare fish in a vast pool, first of all because I was a practitioner and the majority of psychologists were academics. On top of this, the other practitioners specialised mainly in the clinical field and worked in the NHS, whereas I was "occupational", working in every other kind of organisation except the NHS. In the occupational division, I specialised in "development", whereas the majority were into "assessment". I didn't meet other psychologists like me, but I didn't mind because I was enjoying a broad base of colleagues. I reminded myself that some of the most interesting psychologists were heretics, like Carl Rogers and Ronnie Laing, admired for seeing beyond the boundaries of the profession.

I started cutting my own path. I was a coach to leaders and a facilitator to teams, and I started writing articles about it. In 1992, I started to keep a diary, which was initially intended to be a professional log, but soon I was writing more broadly on both the personal and professional matters concerning me. I was making reflective writing a form of personal supervision: my "self" appearing on the page revealed an inner world of thoughts and feelings I barely recognised and failed to express elsewhere. The everyday conundrums of a busy freelancer, new to fatherhood, trying to be a good family man were eased. With direct personal experience of Dad's struggles with work-life balance, I was grateful to have writing as a supervisory prop. I wrote a couple of books. Additional support came from non-psychologists: in my learning set, in the network of developers I co-founded, and in regular co-coaching sessions with colleagues.

By the time I gained the Society's gold standard Chartered status, I realised how closely those two sides of ourselves, professional and personal, are linked. The diary-writing habit of many years made this obvious, but all this time I remained unaware that Dad, also an Organisational Development Consultant but without formal qualifications, wrote a diary.

In the later years of my active working life, I supported a younger Chartered colleague with supervision through one-to-one sessions allowing him to review his practice. We made it reciprocal instead of paid, dividing each session equally, giving each one the support of another experienced colleague.

My surprise in these supervision sessions was to discover within me a story that was clamouring to be told. I needed to write the story of Dad, but I put it off until I had the time to do him justice.

## 2. Storytelling as Therapy

The act of storytelling is curative and therapeutic. I'm wondering why that might be, and how we can better harness this in our work as professionals.

At dinner parties and social events, when asked for my profession, I often say *'Facilitator'*, because when I answer *'Psychologist'* it clams people up. Then they will often check: *'Are you a therapist?'* When I say: *'No, I work with teams and leaders in organisations'*, they will often, with a sigh of relief, offload a personal story.

I understand that caution, but it's a big help to be able to tell our stories. When we've been through any kind of accident we need to tell someone, and then we feel better. Many of us know this, and I'm not the only one who's had no one to tell. If during certain lurid events as a teenager I'd been offered counselling or therapy, I would have refused, because there was a stigma. I wanted to be like my friends, not nutty, not having a "nervous breakdown". I was strong enough to withstand my lurid events.

Like many people, I am still hesitant about therapy, favouring friend-to-friend help, self-help, and co-coaching. I want to be on a level playing field, avoiding mumbo-jumbo. Dad's life might have contributed to this aversion, because I saw him suffer various unreliable therapies. I watched The Human Potential Movement excite and embolden him, messing up his judgement.

When later, for reasons inexplicable to me, I followed Dad as an Organisational Development Consultant, one look at him showed me that therapy can be dangerous. He seemed to be part of a cult, and the surrounding secrecy was part of the problem.

During our professional formation, we will all be weighing up what to get involved with. I was ruling out therapy and biasing myself against secrecy. I looked for transparent not mysterious routes towards understanding. My route needed to be safer than Dad's: via university, getting Chartered and patently professional. Since my path didn't cross much with psychologists, and I didn't bring psychology home, I became one who stood back and poked things with long sticks, believing

scepticism was healthy, and blind faith could turn me into Dad.
I kept a rough mental map of what was on offer, marked up with
where I would and wouldn't go.

Through this cautious approach, I discovered at some point that
narrative, or storytelling could bring some of the benefits of
therapy, with greater simplicity and transparency. To explain this
I need to define those terms and give some examples. The term
"therapy" can be defined in many different ways, but let's say
it amounts to: *giving the client a new perspective to handle the
challenges in their life.*

To illustrate, here is a brief form of therapy from my cousin's
training as a health clinician in Australia. They call the method
"Santa's Sack" and it's offered for dealing with a distressed or
complaining patient. The clinician takes the patient to a quiet
place for as long as it takes, up to a couple of hours, asking the
patient to offload their troubles as if from an invisible sack of
presents, one by one. The patient will bring out bereavements,
botched treatments, the bad manners of a doctor or the
unacceptable waiting times. During this unloading the clinician
says nothing except *'Uh huh'* and *'Is there anything else?'* When
the patient's sack is empty, the clinician says: *'OK, let's go over
what we've found'.* As the clinician plays back a summary, the
patient will visibly relax, perhaps letting out a small sigh of relief.
Only then is the patient ready for to discuss the options and to
make choices about how to proceed. It's brief, it's client-centred
therapy, and it gives the client a new perspective.

Having settled on those few words to define what therapy is,
the benefit in writing and telling stories becomes more obvious:
it gets things off our chests, and lets the fog clear. I once
initiated a project with colleagues in which I invited them to
write about their personal transitions from one job or life phase
into the next. We assembled their stories into a collection,
circulated it amongst the other writers and held a workshop
to reflect on the impact of writing and telling their stories.
During this project I learned that Narrative Therapy encourages
people to create the stories that support them in making
transitions. More recently, through the direct experience of
writing as a son about his father, I'm all too aware of the power
of such methods for surfacing denied material, and opening up

a new perspective.

When we seek to use our stories in a therapeutic way, we find our stories are never entirely about us. Much of their value is in illuminating our relations with friends, partners, colleagues and adversaries, in our families, workplaces, as part of some larger group or tribe or society. Through exploring the present yearning and the possible future story we can adjust our position. Through telling such stories, we offer colleagues a chance to reflect on their own positions.

When long ago in 1928, Margaret Mead wrote about the tribes she observed in Samoa, she was criticised for being insufficiently rigorous and objective in her ethnographic recording, but today we believe that nothing can be observed in social science without an "observer effect". Interestingly, in therapy the observer effect is exactly what we're seeking to harness: the act of writing produces that phenomenal effect, when it causes us and others to reflect. With the birth of a new field in the 1970s called "auto-ethnography" the writer does not even try to be objective about a client or tribe or society ("the other") because their own personal feelings and reflections ("the self") are acknowledged as the lens through which they study the tribe. This offers us a different door to enter the field of therapy: reflecting on ourselves while also bringing these reflections into our conversations with those around us.

In summary, I've come to believe that when we help our clients tell their stories, and pay good attention while they do, that can be therapeutic for all concerned. It allows helping professionals to cut away mumbo-jumbo. We can make the drawing out of clients' stories, and the writing by clients of their own stories integral to our practice. We must think carefully about how widely we share the stories, but sometimes, something personal like a story can be used to embolden others who wish they could contribute more.

There's another benefit for helping professionals in developing their narrative method. Every helping professional (counsellor, coach, clergy, consultant, nurse, health ancillary) finds themselves dealing with a distressed client at one time or another, and needs a method like the Santa's Sack (above). This illustrates how our work contains a tension between our own needs as professionals and the needs of another. It is "me" versus "you" versus "us". We might address that tension by falling back on accepted professional standards, conscience, loyalties, beliefs and values, but there is always difficulty for a professional who is reconciling these conflicts.

When people need us to help, we set boundaries, and reflect on where we draw the lines. We can be neglectful of ourselves, or overconfident of our capabilities. Without sufficient investment in support and reflection, our responsibilities start to weigh too heavily on us, bringing stress and possible burnout.

On top of this professional challenge, the scale of need out there is growing. We're just mopping up the kitchen floor, with little effect, while a flood is pouring in. We need to multiply our reach and impact, and this requires us to scrutinise our methods and find ways to evolve.

Let's call to mind the story of where our profession started, and track its trajectory. A century of psychology has given rise to many professions (therapist, consultant, coach, facilitator) and a "therapising" or "Americanising" of the traditional ones (teacher, doctor, nurse). There's always a therapeutic dimension when a professional works with a client, and there's always a need for the professional to participate in evolving their profession.

The next section seeks to draw on the value of story, to describe the water we're swimming in, which for brevity I've labelled the "cult of self". With our context described, we're better able to consider our choices.

## 3. The "Cult of Self" and What's Coming Next

A "Cult of Self" was evidently emerging in the Sixties, not just for Dad. There was a huge upside: a wave of individualism was washing through society, bringing a remarkable new urge for individuals to live less stunted lives. At home I experienced the destructive side of this cult and, when you believe a cult is destroying your family, naturally you gave this topic a wide birth. But I admit to my curiosity about what exactly was going on, and what gave rise to it. Over the years I've been able to assemble the story, and I believe that my fellow professionals can benefit from keeping this history in mind.

Since the start of time we have been learning who we are and who we can be. We began to hunt, but when 10,000 years ago we shifted to tilling the land we had to organise ourselves, and defend the crops. Then we were constantly re-organising ourselves with wars, armies, conquerors, slavery, religion, democracy, and all kinds of revolutions. Each re-organisation brought a different way to live and work together.

The Industrial Revolution arose after the printing press and the Enlightenment produced an explosion of new knowledge. Factories spawned communities of workers who, in poor conditions, produced cheap goods using better and better machines. Profit flowed to the owners, fuelling the engineering advances that drove the ships, cars and aeroplanes which expanded our horizons. But the new machines cast huge numbers out of work, producing social upheaval with "luddites" fighting the advances. New social movements sought to improve working conditions. The continuing answer to how to organise was "get big": large centralised organisations (like General Motors, the Catholic Church and the Red Army) overtook the enthusiastic local amateurs. Max Weber introduced orderly bureaucracy with specific jobs, defined rights and obligations, authority levels, supervision and subordination, written rules, and recruitment based on competence. The rules applied to all, regardless of privilege, status, family or religion.

For the last 100 years, an astonishingly pervasive disruption has left no person untouched, for example the world wars, the religious decline, growth of science and technology, economic progress, world travel, telecommunications, computing, social media… and therapy. Each new wave has carried new challenges and new people into our scene, requiring us to reconsider ourselves: *'what's going on?'*, *'who are they?'*, *'so who am I again?'* Our questions might have softened to engage with the "new arrivals": *'who are you?'*, and *'and who are we?'* By redefining self, identity, family, loyalty and belonging, we re-clarify the boundary between me and you, or us and them. It is all about tribe and cult, and being human.

The "cult" is an extreme form: a group of people sharing a fierce interest perhaps as innocent as a fashion for tight trousers, or as difficult as anti-social acts, suicide and murder. The "cult of self" we are about to examine is not so extreme: it is a group that coalesced around certain desires that some outsiders found troubling. When we look back through 21st century eyes, this cult's tendency to celebrate "self" without equal interest in "other" looks over-blown, outdated and unbalanced.

If we look over human history, madness was always expressed in brutality, amidst domestic, tribal or religious wars. The Enlightenment brought secularity, scepticism and rationalism and with it a loss of security and morality, and fuelled an "age of anger". The Industrial Revolution added to this by ripping apart families and communities throughout Europe. The forces unleashed were powerful, producing deep disturbance in individuals including fear, depression, hysteria and aggression.

Early in the twentieth century, to address those psychic disturbances, Psychoanalysis was developed by Freud and Jung and others, but it failed to address the wider causes of madness in society. Jung's focus was on "individuation" and he said life was a journey through which we discover who we truly are, as distinct individuals. Such "solutions for the self" reached only a tiny privileged minority, while the rise of war-mongering dictators was producing death and trauma on an industrial scale.

After Psychoanalysis was criticised as unscientific, Behaviourism (Pavlov, Watson, Skinner) followed, but failed to provide the deeper insights about ourselves that people craved. Asylums remained full with inmates diagnosed as "neurotic" or "psychotic", who were offered a wide range of treatments including lobotomies, electro-convulsion, the chemical cosh, and group therapy. The neurotics tended to recover regardless of treatment (c. 70% spontaneous remission in two years), and there were plenty more to take their place, while the Psychotics tended to require long-term treatment and rarely recovered.

The appetite post-Second World War was to understand the grotesque wartime behaviour (loss of moral qualms, mass hysteria and brutality) and US psychologists researched authoritarianism (Prof. Philip Zimbardo), conformity (Prof. Solomon Asch) and obedience (Prof. Stanley Milgram), while the US Military funded research into group dynamics as a defence against fascism and communism. This work confirmed that individuals can be manipulated to go along with the boss or the crowd, often against their own best interests, and transgressing widely accepted moral standards. This taught us about the importance of holding onto our boundaries between self, dictator and crowd.

In 1948, The United Nations General Assembly in Paris set out a fundamental standard of human rights, for all peoples and all nations. These included life, liberty and security, freedom of speech and belief, and education towards the full development of the personality.

In 1961, Psychology moved forward in a bold new direction with the first issue of a Journal of Humanistic Psychology. Dr Abraham Maslow, a respected psychologist, wrote about a new zeitgeist that questioned the place of "objectivity" in the study of human nature. Maslow traced the growth of psychology naming Psychoanalysis as the "first force", followed by Behaviourism (instead of talking from the couch, this relied on scientific manipulations of behaviour using rewards or punishments) as the "second force". Maslow criticised both "forces" for their focus on illness instead of health, and proposed Humanistic Psychology as a "third force". This called for the study of real human experience, with the aim of liberating people from the "bonds of neurotic control" whether from the outside (the strictures of our society, family or job) or the inside (problems inside ourselves). There were echoes of Jung's "individuation" and Maslow believed that with such liberation, human beings might at last set aside the foolish distinctions between good and evil that kept sending us into war.

The idea of being liberated by humanism was obviously attractive to those whose lives entailed conforming and following orders, but liberation was a big word. Historically, most of us had never been kings or queens entitled to be themselves, and any freedoms were within very narrow margins. We expected to surrender our selfish interests for the greater good, making ourselves anonymous in great hoards, serving those with greater power than ourselves. We took orders, and if we rebelled in the war we expected to be shot dead. We wanted to be free, and to be "me", to speak, to express and create, to give and take, to influence and decide and choose, to perform and to relax after the performance.

But I wonder what are the sensible limits to liberty? What are our duties to others in a peaceful and civilised society? How safe do we feel driving along a crowded motorway when all the drivers are liberated and no one follows a Highway Code? This brings us back to the UN Declaration of Human Rights, and the question of our responsibilities towards one another.

Going back to Maslow, his research into peak experiences (the moments we are at our best), defined five fundamental human needs (basic food and warmth etc, safety, love and belonging, esteem and self-actualisation) that when satisfied will remove anxiety, and create an appetite to grow to our greater potential.

Instead of Maslow, many people considered Aldous Huxley the true father of the Human Potential Movement. Huxley's 1960 talk at the University of California in San Francisco Medical Center pointed to our untapped potentials as human beings: *'The neurologists have shown us that no human being has ever made use of as much as ten percent of all the neurones in his brain. And perhaps, if we set about it in the right way, we might be able to produce extraordinary things out of this strange piece of work that a man is'.*

Huxley called for an institution that could teach these "human potentialities", and in 1962 he visited Big Sur (California) where Michael Murphy and Dick Price were opening Esalen Institute, a centre for the development of human potential to initiate a global Human Potential Movement (HPM).

To enter the Esalen campus either as guru or discipline required a leap of faith. You were wrapping yourself in a great utopian blanket. They called it a "religion of no religion". Three distinct groups began to assemble there: bodyworkers (followers of Reich and Rolf, with macrobiotic diets, and bio-energetic therapies), truth seekers (following Aldous Huxley, Abraham Maslow, Carl Rogers, and Eastern religions) and so-called politicos (adherents of the Civil Rights Movement, feminism and anti-war).

Gurus from those three groups soon fell into fierce competition and open enmity, in part because their income depended on attracting followers. All the biggest names practised at Esalen. Fritz Perls' events were nicknamed "circuses", and his acolytes ridiculed Abraham Maslow's intellectuals. William Schulz's gang called themselves the "flying circus" in an effort to outdo Perls. Esalen suffered from all sorts of scandals not only because the therapists and gurus would prey sexually on their clients, but also because Timothy Leary brought LSD there, and every famous figure from the Sixties counter-culture paid a visit.

In August 1963, Maslow and his followers formed the American Association for Humanistic Psychology with a founding meeting in Philadelphia of 100 delegates. They created *'an active organisation'* with *'officers, goals and problems',* concerned with understanding what it means to be human. Abraham Maslow is remembered as one of the three founders, alongside Carl Rogers, best known as a psychotherapist, and Virginia Satir, a family therapist who also become prominent at Esalen.

The new Association for Humanistic Psychology (AHP for short, they dropped the word American) became the standard bearer for HPM as it rapidly spread its influence globally through conferences, the Journal of Humanistic Psychology, its training institutes and personal growth centres which sprung up throughout the world.

In 1969, the AHP opened in Britain with a "growth centre" and a programme of "open experiential events" in London. Fifty to sixty people attended each event, and the mailing list soon grew to 500. A further boost was provided in 1970 when gurus from Esalen visited London and ran two large events at the Inn on the Park.

By today's standards, the Esalen, HPM and AHP gurus were crazy and unprincipled, but in the Sixties their iconoclastic approach was considered liberating. Dad for example was drawn to Maslow, Rogers, Perls, Schulz and also to a bio-energetic faction. As one of the early AHP members in Britain, Dad met Roger Harrison, an American consultant who provided the "Blocks to Creativity" (that he carried in our white camper van to Germany in 1972). Harrison noticed that Humanistic Psychology was regarded with suspicion in Britain. Some called it an American cult that was distorting the beliefs of its followers. A letter from Harrison reflected on these trans-Atlantic differences.

*To International AHP Newsletter, San Francisco, Summer 1972*

*I've had a few diagnostic comments on AHP people when they visit us in Europe, which might cast a light on the difficulties (not necessarily in order of importance).*

- *Americans come as missionaries, to teach rather than to learn. They talk and demonstrate, but they don't ask and listen much.*
- *Americans are socially confident, forward and outgoing. Naturally they make social mistakes and frequently appear to Europeans as naïve and superficial. Rarely will a European help an American by pointing this out.*
- *Americans in the humanistic movement are focussing primarily on the individual. By contrast the developments in Europe are with social systems to do with authority, freedom and power.*
- *Europeans are deferential to visiting Americans, and don't speak much about what they're doing, so the Americans don't recognise that valuable things are being done here.*
- *Europeans distrust American gimmickry, especially when it is put forward on a pragmatic basis ('it works so let's use it and worry about the theory later').*
- *Europeans are hesitant at organising and running things. They aren't as "organisational".*
- *Europeans are envious of the money that Americans have to organise conventions, to make foreign trips; to educate themselves.*
- *Many creative and active Europeans feel they don't really belong in the humanistic movement.*

*I hope that the above may help in some small way to explain what I think has been a problem not only in England but in parts of Europe as well. These remarks should not be taken as questioning the sincerity of any of the Americans who have been engaged in the attempt to internationalise AHP.*

*Roger Harrison, 35 Abbington Court, London, W8.*

Despite Harrison's reservations, HPM and the membership of AHP in Britain continued to grow.

At the same time a transatlantic Anti-Psychiatry Movement was growing, made up of disillusioned clinicians. R D Laing was a Scottish psychiatrist regarded by some as a maverick and by many as the figurehead of that Movement. According to its doctrine, the insane were scapegoats of the families whose impossible rules ("double binds") created their insanity. Their mission was to over-turn the myth of mental illness by putting an end to the labelling of psychiatric conditions and by letting clinicians live alongside patients, without obvious rules or hierarchy, claiming a journey into madness could make you a wiser and more grounded person.

In 1972, Laing's therapeutic community was falling apart while clinicians were dosing themselves freely with alcohol and LSD. Some said Laing's brilliant mind had gone wrong, and he was certainly facing severe financial difficulties when he took advantage of his continuing popularity in the US with a lecture tour. There he met Elizabeth Fehr, a midwife turned psychotherapist, and on his return to London put together a team to run "rebirthing workshops" in which a client assisted by a group of helpers could re-experience the struggle of trying to break out of a birth canal.

The behaviour of the gurus in HPM was regarded by many as mad and self-serving, despite those gurus' claims to be releasing people from crushing conformity. The critics did not buy Carl Jung's argument for individuation, any more than they bought Maslow's argument for liberation, or Huxley's for human potential. They used the term "narcissism" defined by Sigmund Freud in 1914 as the condition of "loving oneself". They noted that Freud said this condition was normal for a two year old, but in adults it was mental illness. They observed the gurus' inflated sense of their own importance as the spreading contagion of narcissism.

The "concern for other" never had an easy relationship with "concern for self". It was an old argument that had been rumbling on for hundreds of years. In the mid-nineteenth century a sociologist Auguste Comte called for "altruism", in other words caring selflessly about the welfare of others, and acting to help other people. Others argued against Comte saying many problems in the world stem from altruism. Long before Comte, Adam Smith maintained that "sympathy" was not sensible without "self-interest": *'It is not from the benevolence of the butcher, the brewer or the baker that we expect our dinner, but from their regard to their own interest'*. It was not only the economists who followed Adam Smith's promotion of "healthy narcissism".

By the 1960s, none of that history much mattered because altruism was passé, particularly to adherents of the Human Potential Movement, because their own desires for individuality and creative expression were so overwhelming. They were caught up in an anti-authoritarian zeitgeist. Dad, once a generous and religious man, entranced by this "cult of self-gratification" (my auntie's term), was determined at whatever cost to escape the chains of conformity. Personal Growth workshops were all the rage, promising to attendees delicious fests of free speech, feedback, laughing, crying, hugging, and in some cases, nakedness and promiscuity.

With the arrival of the 1970s, an economic depression was replacing the heady optimism of the 1960s. By the start of the 1980s, Britain's priority was financial growth rather than personal growth. Harsh economic medicine, monetarism, cuts in spending, a wave of privatisation, with the sale of public housing and the smashing of trades unions, made money the new religion, and widened the wealth gap, with increasing levels of greed and envy.

The fall of the Berlin Wall in 1989 unleashed into previously communist countries the full force of a triumphant market economy. As this spread into developing countries, powerful counter-currents of resentment arose amongst those who gained little from capitalism.

By the start of the twenty-first century, individuality and greed, combined with spreading resentment, provided fertile conditions for narcissism. California, whose self-gratifying Human Potential Movement swept the western world in the Sixties, was about to produce a second hurricane called social media (Facebook, Twitter, Instagram). The ripples would spread to every person on the planet, causing hundreds of millions of people to broadcast their glossy sides, burying their less commendable features. The unintended impact on billions of others was to produce envy and depression.

With this background to our work as psychologists today, we can see that the individualism that was so liberating in the Sixties is producing levels of narcissism that Freud might have classed as mental illness. In the news every day, further evidence arrives of once unified societies splintering into factions, unleashing envy and hatred against former compatriots. The consequent turmoil adds to the insecurity that creates today's extreme politics, migration, terrorism and war. We are living in post-globalisation chaos.

As helping professionals what do we want to do about it? Would we rather turn a blind eye? Would we confine ourselves like Freud and Jung to solutions for the self? Or do we consider it our business to reflect on society, or to start new methods and movements? What can we offer to those in governance?

But isn't it tempting to start afresh, with a blank sheet of paper?

# 4. When Rebirthing Is Wishful Thinking, and When It Isn't

There's a method called "rebirthing" that came out of the Sixties. It makes you think you can draw a line and leave the past behind. I first heard about it from my Dad.

Dad's surprise return before Christmas in 1974 raised a lot of questions, because two years earlier he had walked out. After Christmas I was driving back to university, and he asked me for a lift to his new home in the north of England. During the three-hour journey, he was unusually talkative. He asked about my Psychology course and my dissertation on Recovery From Mental Illness. Had I heard of R D Laing, the famous psychiatrist? I said no. He suggested I look into Laing's work, and went on to describe a "rebirthing" experience he had recently undergone with Laing, which had affected him deeply: *'Everyone has nasty memories they would rather forget. Laing's method lets you wipe the slate clean and start afresh. It's a physical thing, nothing to do with talking'*.

*'How well did it work?'*
*'I certainly felt better afterwards'*.

Dad's answer was cagey, and naturally I was sceptical. To my mind the rebirthing was Dad's way of dodging certain conflicts rather than working things out properly.

Several years passed before I became curious about rebirthing. Then I dug around on the Internet and found links to Laing's colleagues and family. Laing's son, Adrian described a trial rebirthing session in which he was a guinea pig: *'We were in an old church hall in Belsize Park... (Dad's) helpers were all dressed in pastel-coloured tracksuits and emitting a ... unified moaning noise. They surrounded me at my back, at my hips, at my shoulders and at my head, where they pushed hands down on me to simulate a womb opening. I had to push to get out from between them while they tried to stop me. The idea was to relive the struggle I had had to be born'*.

As Laing developed the method, his rebirthings became more intense, tribal, intimate, cathartic and ritualistic.

When I heard there was a play about Laing staged in Dalston in 2015, I wished I had been able to attend, and I imagined the rebirthing scene it might (but almost certainly didn't) include.

\*

- **Setting:** 2015, Arcola Theatre, Dalston
- **Props:** Door, small light, flesh coloured suits
- **Characters:** Ronnie, Dad, 10 helpers

On the dot of seven-thirty, we dash into the small theatre in Dalston. This intimate space, without a stage as such, is surrounded on three sides by ninety chairs. A hush signals the play is about to start, and we tiptoe self-consciously to two remaining seats: front and dead centre. All eyes are on us, until the actors appear.

The stage is empty except for a door propped open at the far right hand corner. This is supposed to be a church hall.

Ronnie, the skinny, bearded psychiatrist, walks across the empty hall and opens the door to an overweight middle-aged man standing in the "foyer". Ronnie offers his hand. The man puts down a heavy briefcase. His face is sweating. Ronnie gives him a glass of water, and sends him off-stage to empty his bladder.

A moment later, the man returns looking more comfortable and Ronnie's briefing begins: *'You push hard to be born again, while all life's accretions prevent you. Only through struggle is re-birth possible. It's a visceral process, drawing out painful memories stored in the tissue. Your old life familiar but horribly restrictive, is like a womb closing in, because you have outgrown it. To be born into a new world promises to bring what is currently denied to you. You will start afresh, freed completely from the past.*

*'It is not like the River Jordan, in fact not religious at all. It's not about believing anything, nor talking or thinking anything. Your release arises directly out of your struggle. You are to give this matter no further thought, and you are to remain silent throughout. Any questions?'*

No. So Ronnie continues: *'When you enter the hall, it will be*

*empty. You will move towards the small light, and stop in the
centre of the space. Helpers will surround you. You have to get
between the Helpers into a birth canal, and just keep pushing
until you emerge at the far end'.*

The man removes his jacket, shoes and tie, and then shuffles
through the flimsy door. Half way across he turns towards us,
and taking two large steps, he stares directly at me. His eyes
are scrunched, his head angles slightly to one side, mouth open,
pulled down at the edges, like a sick child, shrinking from a
spoonful of medicine. He looks like Dad.

At first I barely notice the Helpers, in flesh-coloured flying suits
and shiny bathing caps, taking slow choreographed steps, to
surround the poor man, pressing against him with their hands
and bodies. It is dark except for a small lamp on the back wall.
I can make out Helpers climbing on the man's shoulders, and
I feel their weight pushing me down in my seat. Then it is a
battle to sit still because my legs are resisting and pushing me
up.

The Helpers are mingling all around the man, making a low eerie
hum. Instead of helping, they are blocking him, forming a tight
moving wall. He is sticking out hands, grabbing and jabbing,
trying to prise something open. With ten Helpers, the odds are
against him.

They are one solid thing, an organism, rotating, smooth
and serene. The man tries jumping, twisting and flailing his arms,
then the shape loosens to surround him. He leaps out through
a gap, but the thing regroups to capture him again. Defeated he
slumps and the organism continues rotating.

My heart is thumping.

The man desperate now takes this chance to make a violent
attack, slamming a knee into a groin, grabbing a head. But his
hands slide off and he gains nothing. The organism just dances
jauntily on.

The man falls to his knees, and the Helpers squat. He grabs
a Helper's arm, and the Helper grabs him back, then another

Helper joins to swing him round and up and down, fast like a Waltzer. They lay the dizzy man on the ground. The other Helpers lie down in layers and make an opening between their reclined bodies, then his dizzy body finds its way into a tight canal. He must be baking in there.

The Helpers' noise rises to a steady drone, then an extended roar and suddenly it's silent. The man inches forward headfirst. There is a rhythm of wriggling and writhing. The Helpers' voices echo in unison the man's grunts and groans. But as he advances the canal only extends, while the thing slowly rotates in a tense trancelike collaboration.

My feet press down and my hands brace against the seat to support the man's advance. The organism, one moment gently rotating, abruptly stops. A flushed head is poking out towards us. Two Helpers arrive on each side, waving their arms and reaching in to grab the bloated body.

At first, the birth canal sucks back, then the body plops out onto the four Helpers, knocking them off their feet. I leap up. Helen hisses: *'No!'* and grabs my arm. We hunch low.

Four Helpers roughly haul themselves out, letting the head drop hard on the parquet. Sweaty, it shivers.

Ronnie moves in fast, raising his arms like a priest over the new-born, and booms the order: *'Bombard!'* Lights flood the face, with screaming ululations and a deafening pan-lid clatter. At my feet is a spasm of sobbing and Dad's vacant eyes. Sobs rise in me and I freeze myself inside.

The pink helpers recede, unzip their suits and file out in a silent line, leaving Ronnie and his patient. Ronnie offers a chair: *'Sit, settle yourself, and drink this'.* After the eerie speechless play, his words resonate to fill the room, Coldly, without expression, he intones from a slim black book:
*'One feels empty because there is nothing inside oneself.*
*One may think there is a gate to go through, without finding it.*
*There is no gate. No one ever found a gate…'*

In the midst of his bleak message, Ronnie trails off.

Dad speaks up angrily: *'Ronnie, if there was never a gate, what is this Rebirthing for?'* How lost the man is.
*'It is for you to find that out!'* replies Ronnie.
Dad pleads despairingly: *'How is this supposed to help?'*

\*

Before the rebirthing Dad had been stuck. So he was willing to make a leap of faith, and this brought him out of the frying pan into the fire. He couldn't stand the agony of furious daily arguments in his new family on top of the guilt he carried for leaving his old family, but he couldn't turn back the clock. So he needed a magic wand.

The rebirthing session was Dad's Plan A and it emptied him out, but the pain of his divided life soon returned. His Plan B was the return home that Christmas to his old family. Mum swiftly halted the divorce proceedings and agreed to give him one last try, despite the reluctance from her sons. But, by Boxing Day Plan B wasn't working so he hatched Plan C, to try again for the merger of families that everyone had already rejected. For three months Dad flitted then between north and south, trying to broker the merger, until Mum reinstated the divorce. Dad was forced to accept he had failed, and he moved out permanently.

\*

There's an interesting sequel to the rebirthing. Ronnie Laing, who preyed on wishful thinkers as desperate as Dad, was clearly unstable. Four years after Dad's session, Laing's public meeting in August 1978 with Carl Rogers, proved that Laing was getting no better.

Laing's reputation was huge. He had practised at the Tavistock Institute and co-founded the Philadelphia Association to challenge the practice of psychotherapy. His radical writings created a fan base eager to believe that madness is a transformative experience that can produce a wiser and more grounded person.

Rogers, a psychotherapist and founder of humanistic psychology, was widely considered amongst clinicians to be second only to Sigmund Freud. Instead of interpreting the dreams of a recumbent patient, Rogers researched the core conditions required for good therapeutic results (warmth, genuineness and unconditional positive regard). The therapist was a non-judgmental listener, who treated his clients as people not patients and, instead of wild theories, they paid careful attention to the client's reality. He was one who inspired the new industry of coaching.

It was set to be a public debate between two admired men who could learn much from one another. But as it turned out their fundamental differences were starkly exposed.

The two gurus met at Laing's house in Belsize Park the afternoon before the public debate, each surrounded by their small band of acolytes. The room was small, filled with pipe smoke, and marijuana was going round. Laing asked the other side to begin. The Rogerians took turns one after another, followed by a long silence. Rogers delivered his creed about human nature and relationships, but to Laing's followers this was bland and insincere.

Before Rogers could finish Laing interrupted: *'You're going to have to cut out the Californian "nice-guy" act'.*

Carl Rogers, famously a humanist, was always patient and accommodating, and in every important respect different from Laing, the Scotsman, who was said to be nasty, aggressive and often drunk.

Laing seized every opportunity to humiliate Rogers. He invited the Americans for dinner at a nearby Chinese, and they accepted, only to find themselves in more difficult territory. Carl Rogers sat on a long table with everyone else, while Laing, sat alone on a separate table getting drunk. As a customer entered Laing shouted: *'See that bald-headed man sitting there?'* (pointing to Rogers) *'Well he's not a man, he's a pairrrson',* (referring to Rogers' famous book, "On Becoming a Person"). Laing poured a whisky for one of the Rogerians, apparently as a gesture of rapprochement, saying: *'Do you like this?'*, then he spat in the drink saying: *'And do you like it now?'* When confronted about this behaviour, Laing claimed he was happy, and was simply being misunderstood.

Later that night the two groups patched things up.

The following day, in the Grand Ballroom of the London Hilton hotel the turnout of 350 people was less than expected, but nonetheless a significant crowd. Laing introduced Rogers who spoke for a while. When Laing challenged him hard for denying the existence of evil and for the banality of some of his ideas, Rogers failed to muster a defence. The two sat face to face to demonstrate an authentic "encounter" and this went down well with the crowd. Then Laing took a turn to speak and some said he was impossible to follow, until he got up and to the delight of the audience demonstrated, with the aid of several assistants, how to rebirth two hundred people simultaneously, with Laing's full showmanship. This stole the occasion, and there was no more interest in Rogers that day.

Two opposites had produced something explosive. Not everyone considered the day totally disastrous, but there are several competing versions. Most defended their own guru while mauling the other, but at least one publicly recanted and changed sides: this was Maureen O'Hara, who began the meeting as a Rogerian and ended as a supporter of Laing. Rogers was criticised for being spineless and asking to be abused, but Laing's sadistic and aggressive behaviour was said to put his sanity into doubt.

Laing's rebirthing was built on the premise that you can leave yourself behind. Yet the poetry in Laing's book "Knots" belied that: *'There is no gate, no one ever found a gate...'*. Did Laing even believe in rebirthing himself? His writings show that he wanted to be reborn but he found it impossible. Dad also found that out the hard way.

Rogers came from a different point of view: *'We cannot move away from what we are, until we thoroughly accept what we are. Then change seems to come about almost unnoticed'*. That meant you have to begin with self-acceptance (and I'm not sure Dad ever succeeded at that).

Both men had their shortcomings, and after this 1978 meeting Laing and Rogers never spoke to one another again.

*

It is because of Dad's trying to change himself, while hiding from exactly what he was trying to change, that I return to the use of narrative. It makes a lot of sense to start, as Rogers did, from the reality of who and what and where we are. Just saying and writing down the narrative about what we're changing is a good starting point.

Mum displayed this kind of honesty in her letter to Dad in April 1975: *'I tried to be "a good wife" but nothing I could do would make my personality match yours. You struggled with this fact for all our married life, but I came to enjoy what you were rather than hope for you to be different. I hoped that you would be able to see things the same way and enjoy marriage with me as I am, but I understand that you cannot'.*

Here Mum scrapes away the falsehoods about who they are, and where they are in their relationship. She is just describing how it is. She is a generous realist, untangling herself from an optimistic dreamer. Their relationship is as complicated as that between Ronnie Laing (aggressive realist) and Carl Rogers (kindly optimist).

Mum's letter concludes with this: *'I have just spent the evening turning round all the furniture in the lounge and in the course of this thinking that no relationship is lost, whether by death or separation'.*

By then her world is as rearranged as her furniture, bringing her a new perspective, and a release. When we write a letter that clarifies where we are with a partner, and gives a hint about where we're heading, this is a Narrative of Rebirth that is therapeutic and supports our continuing growth.

# 5. Placing Ourselves in System and Society - Five Principles

When my daughter was small, perhaps five years old, I remember her playing with the small stuffed toys she collected, called Beanie Babies. She would make a nest on her duvet and give each baby a place in the circle. She would tell the babies what she was up to that day, and speak to them about each other. I noticed her giving love, confirming each baby's place alongside others, and rehearsing various arguments. Sometimes she would change all of the names and speak to her brother, her friends and even her parents as if we/they were sitting in that circle. Now I notice that what she was working on was a system of human relationships.

For many years, I have been building an understanding of how we can get entangled in the human relationships surrounding us, and how we can untangle or release ourselves. I was interested in the healing of rifts, even before any conscious quest to re-acquaint myself with Dad. A colleague recommended a method called Constellations that derives from family therapy. Of course, for reasons I've already explained, the word "therapy" was a red flag, but this took place in a group rather than one to one. I felt happy to attend a taster day. That day produced insights about how we affect and entrap the other people in our lives, and I remembered the Beanie Babies.

Keen to learn that method, I attended Constellations workshops during the following year. Under the guidance of a tutor, we brought our real examples, and stood in the places of the other people involved in our systems, to speak the truths that came to us. We illuminated the invisible dynamics and hidden loyalties that bedevil us.

I started to apply this method professionally, and the Constellations knowledge profoundly affected how I went about the quest. I was not simply using diaries and old photographs, I was experiencing the traces of those old characters inside me. Using the space on the dining table, and the condiments on the café table in Vienna I felt the tug of those earlier generations and re-enacted their dramas. What I'm about to describe might seem a little strange, but I'm sharing it because it demonstrates, better than I've previously been able, how we can release ourselves from the myopia of self and find a good place in relation to others we seek to influence and upon whom we depend. It happened during a Constellations refresher afternoon in Lewes.

We sat in a circle of eight and the tutor posed a question: *'What system are you in right now?'* She offered her answer as an illustration: *'Until an hour ago I was with a client, so in a "client system", then I stopped in a café, picked up a doughnut and suddenly I was a small child in my "family of origin system" remembering a happy time when my father brought a bag of jam doughnuts home'.*

Then the tutor repeated her question: *'What system are you in right now?'* and we gave our responses: family system, friendship system, retail system, the system in this room, and so on. When my turn came, I said that after a recent big birthday I escaped my "client systems", but flooding into this void came my "family of origin system", with flashbacks about my father. No one looked surprised, but I didn't say any more at the stage.

The point of the tutor's question was obvious: we constantly bring our past systems into the present moment. Next she said something eerily true: *'In any system, when something or someone is excluded the system remembers, literally "re-members"'.*

I gasped inwardly, because we had excluded Dad, and I wondered if the tutor could see deep into my soul. Her words were astoundingly true: the family system had excluded Dad and I was the one who was compelled to re-member him.

Putting aside those inner revelations, I heard the tutor telling us what we can do about this. I wrote it down:

*'When you're in a system where something or someone has been excluded, you need to find a way to acknowledge that thing or that person without judgement, and try to do so kindly'.*

I could hear her stating very clearly what I'd been up to, but I took issue with the *'kindly'* part. I'd tried to be kind for decades, but that "kindness" left the pain inside me. When faced with the choice of ignoring Dad or re-including him and bringing his uncomfortable failures to light, I'd chosen the latter. Was this unkind?

It was "kindness" that threw me off the track, keeping the family system unbalanced, and with the quest I'd taken a different approach. With opening the box, dark things were brought into the light, making it possible finally to join up the dots.

The tutor showed us in that circle in Lewes that we each dragged big invisible sacks of experience behind us, from all the systems we've ever belonged to. Those heavy sacks could become angels wings when we used our experience properly, or so she believed.

What's in the sack is a hidden capacity to understand what's going on in the present, and to make better decisions towards the future. Our key to this is a "felt sense" in our body, from the temperature, skin and muscle sensations, the intensity, and our sense of expansion or constriction. This is called "Somatics". When we declare the information held in our body, as a "sentence of truth" then everything clicks into place. You know it when it happens.

Rather than take this on trust, we asked for a demonstration. The group constellation that followed provided a vivid and memorable example. "Sue" was a member of our group who offered the example. She wanted to answer her question about how to move forward in a particular personal relationship, and invited five of us as representatives to "constellate" her question. Without letting us ask for any more details, the tutor showed us how.

I want you to imagine the five of us standing in a space surrounded by a circle of chairs. I was representing Sue, and the real Sue placed me facing a chap who was representing her partner, P. We were two feet apart. Behind P were two people representing P's Past. Behind me was a woman representing Sue's Past. I could feel her breathing to the left of my neck. Sue herself was sitting nearby in the circle, watching us.

The tutor came to me for a "sentence of truth" about the system. I said: *'It feels crowded here. My toes are twitchy and I have a cramp in my right calf'*. I could feel Sue's Past behind me and I wanted to get away. I looked at P, and sensed that P wanted to escape too, from the strong pull of his past which was lurking behind him.

The tutor went to the others, and P said he needed space. When the tutor went to the woman behind me who represented Sue's Past, she declared that she was angry because I refused to look at her.

In that instant, I had something I had to say to P: *'We both want to leave the past behind, and I'm not sure it is possible'.*
P replied wearily: *'I just want space'.*
P appeared to want the space more than he wanted me.

Then Sue spoke from her seat in the circle: *'This is all unbelievably true, but it doesn't give me a way forward'.*

So far we were depicting the status quo, and the tutor briefed us on a curious next step: *'Now I want all the representatives to make "one move towards better"'.*

With that, P stepped away to his left, distancing himself from the two characters in his past, continuing to face me, but further away. I stepped diagonally to my right bringing me slightly closer to P but distancing myself from the past at my back. I also turned 45 degrees making it possible for me to see both P and my past at a single glance.

When the tutor checked in with us, P was much more comfortable and, as soon as he said that, so was I.
But the woman representing my past gave me a hard look and addressed me: *'You're still not looking at me'.*
I replied: *'I have turned to look'.*
She said: *'But you're not looking kindly'.*

I could feel a heavy tension in my chest and stomach, as if I was defending myself. I took a deep breath and tried to soften my expression, but my mouth only twitched and refused to smile.

Some words came to me and I spoke these as a proposal to the woman: *'If I try to look kindly on you, will you will look kindly on me?'* My eye contact was direct and deliberate.

The face of the woman repenting my past softened slightly. She replied: *'I will try'* with a tremor in her voice.

This had a powerful effect, which I reported to the tutor in a "sentence of truth": *'My eyes just welled up and my defences melted. It feels like we've been released'.*

As I said that, I became calm and my face relaxed easily into a smile. The conflict was over. I was making friends with the past, and feeling at peace.

The tutor asked me to step out of the circle, and walk round the room to loosen up, and as I did so I reflected. The exchange I had just been part of was actually nothing to do with me. Yes I was intimately involved, I'd felt the feelings and said the words, but they were not mine, because I was just a representative for Sue.

Leaving Lewes that afternoon on the train, I felt as if I was floating. I played a Nick Mulvey album through my earphones and the lyrics (about remembering, about secrets, and about when the body is gone) seemed to describe the constellation I'd just left, and brought me back somehow to Dad.

I was like a child representing many children. It was crowded and I was looking across at Dad whose past was behind him. He was stepping away, so I took a step to keep up with him, but he frowned back with irritation. I kept him in my sights as I half turned to check what was behind me. Then I saw Mum standing there and looking after me, my sister and brothers with her. I looked back with warmth, and Mum's worried expression softened. She was trusting me to go after Dad, because he needed someone with him.

As the train rattled towards Clapham Junction, I felt my family truth had been clarified, just as we had illuminated Sue's truth earlier that afternoon. I remembered how undeniably real it was when my eyes welled up earlier, then my eyes welled up again. I sensed that my family system was rebalancing, and it was a sign I'd done my work.

I guessed the Lewes constellation was archetypal, because on the train such similar steps explained my release from the absent people (including Dad, Mum, my sister) who used to tie me in knots. These things can't ever be fixed, but the tension is gone and the 'Constellation lets us manage any set of relationships to be less disruptive.

I'm noticing the time this whole journey took: from my sixtieth birthday to writing this story in the first person was about two years, which was once claimed to be the time taken for spontaneous remission. Those inexplicable recoveries from neuroses, without treatment, were explained (possibly naively) in my undergraduate thesis, as due to "psychotherapeutic agents in the community", in other words, the love of friends and family.

*

Just before Abraham Maslow died in 1970, he glimpsed the limits of self-liberation. He called for a "fourth force" in psychology that he named "transpersonal" (strengthening the bonds between self and other) and a "fifth force" that he named "universal" (addressing the human need for meaning).

Maslow's final revelation wasn't clear to most people. He was an atheist so he wasn't calling everyone to church. Had he just been smoking weed? No one knows, but we're pointed to the conclusion that psychology and society had to move beyond the obsession with self. Maslow was asking us to move from "me" to focus "you" and "us".

I've come to believe that these two extra human needs (for social bonds and a sense of shared meaning) highlighted by Maslow might provide us as helping professionals with a hint of how to tackle the post-globalisation crises (financial crash, splintering of nations, migration, terrorism, wars, the prospect of widespread automation etc) in which we are all mired.

The meeting in Lewes reminded me that the huge challenges surrounding us in this chaotic era can only be solved in cooperation with others. The practice of Constellations shows us a way to put this into practice.

*

The morning after my trip to Lewes I awoke with a clear head and the sun was shining. I was looking forward to a walk in the countryside with Helen. First I spent an hour noting down ideas about how people function, which had arisen in the constellation session. I called these "principles for finding our place in the system".

**1. Growing up.** I believe we all have a child inside. Studies with mothers and infants testify to a "reciprocity" that is universal and permeates all human experience: baby cries, mother gives food, baby gurgles, mother smiles, and so on. No baby survives without interacting, and grows up "co-producing" unique two-way exchanges for mutual benefit. This "reciprocity" dance teaches us tuning in and actively engaging, to take up our place in a system of relations to others.

**2. System Belonging.** In Lewes we experienced a lively flow when the system was balanced, giving everyone a place, honouring those who came before, enabling a two-way exchange of giving and receiving. It's like an ecosystem with everyone connected and interdependent, like plants and animals in a forest.

Starting in our family of origin, we all develop unspoken rules and hidden loyalties because we need to belong, My family of origin gave me: behave well, share, don't make a fuss, don't cry, don't get angry, tell the truth and don't tell tales. It's not necessary or healthy to hold onto these rules all through life, because in every new system we enter, there are different rules we must follow if we want to belong.

**3. Stumbling.** No one's perfect, and no human system is ever stable. Our daily reciprocity dances are beset with stumbles, misunderstandings and crippling feelings. We face personal challenges and system threats, sparking fight and flight reactions, blocking the flow, like a kink or a rupture in a hose. Any blockage raises the risk of breaking the rules and being excluded, while of course we still yearn to belong.

Constellation practice shows us that past ruptures leave a

mark that is hard to discuss because of the unspoken rules, loyalties and shame. But unless we illuminate the rupture, and do so kindly without blame or judgement, the truth becomes "excluded" and thereafter will be "re-membered", but in a way that hijacks us.

**4. Disabling Sickness.** Those of us born into a hierarchical world have experienced family and work systems based on silence, violence and blame, which refuse to be illuminated or repaired. We can call these sick systems because they produce secrets (eg. withheld information, ignorance, incompetence), sickness (eg. heart disorders, eating disorders), and insanity (eg. displacement, exclusion, loss, stress, distress, obsession, dependency, narcissism, psychosis), and a stream of clients for teachers, medics and therapists.

But when a helping profession treats the individual not the sick system, this raises a provocative question:

*How can we release a person from the system*
*that holds him or her in an unhealthy entanglement?*

**5. Finding Our Place.** Our cluster of helping professions is divided into the person-oriented (psychology, nursing, doctors, therapists) and the system-oriented (community leaders, sociologists, social workers, schools leaders, politicians, governance and government). It's rare to find colleagues who address both the client and the system that makes their client feel stuck.

Johann Muller's thirty-year record at Villa Lilly for releasing crack addicts from their addiction is an outstanding example of how to go further than simply treating the individual. His aim is for the individual to sustain themselves in society without drugs, instead of retreating into self-medication. At Villa Lilly, the clients are given real jobs and the means to try out living in new ways while up against the hidden loyalties and troublesome rules of belonging to that community. Johann jumps on any hint of cynicism about the regime because cynicism erodes everyone's belief. He shows addicts how to stand up again, and over many months to build up the strength to look him honestly in the eye. Then they return safely into society.

In each helping profession the specifics may be different. How can doctors adequately address today's chaos with anti-depressants? How can a school adequately address today's chaos within the current lesson plan, and the existing school culture? I've spent a career working in the business of developing the leaders and teams that run quite large organisations, and from this perspective such questions come to mind.

When we pause to take in the context surrounding our work as helping professionals one thing is clear: there will never be enough helping professionals to meet the demand, because the post-globalisation crises are stretching and fracturing our systems. With more and more clients arriving, we'll always be bogged down in hopeless cases and, until we can work with the systems producing our clients, how can we stem the flow?

Instead of promising liberation, mustn't we now question our assumptions? In doing so, we raise questions not only for the helping professions, but for community leaders and government. How can we share, and how can we enable each other to thrive, particularly as cities get more crowded? How can we match the unleashed individualism with an equal portion of care towards others?

As helpers, it can feel as if we are in the same boat as our clients: powerless, and susceptible to despair. It's a cliché to say we must think outside the box, but as professionals don't we need to come together, to find the relevant responses and reinvent the rules?

Here are three closing questions that perhaps offer hope whether you're a clinician, social worker or therapist, whether you're delivering a baby, running a school or building a team:

- *What if we can illuminate, and help to rebalance the systems that give rise to our clients' (pupils' patients' etc) needs?*

- *What if our clients could learn how to find their right place in those systems?*

- *What if the education system could turn out adults with self-in-system understanding?*

# Notes and Sources

## Chapter 5: Peak Bubble
The midlife crisis was first recognised in the Sixties, but recently there is a growing understanding of early and later life crises:
- Oliver Robinson, Later Life Crisis: Towards a Holistic Model, Journal of Adult Development, Vol 1, No3 (https://goo.gl/JWeCLV)

On writing a journal
- Tony Page, Diary of a Change Agent, Gower, 1996

## Chapter 6: Weddings, War Heroes and Wonder Women
- John Duffy, Britain's Secret Sex Survey, BBC News Magazine, 30 Sep 2005 (https://goo.gl/DWSmzF)

Margaret Mead's research in Samoa is said to have inspired new sexual freedoms in the permissive society of the Sixties.
- Jan Howard, Margaret Mead: A Life, Ballantine, 1989

## Chapter 7: Humpback Bridges
Studies of Autobiographical Memory show that people vary in their capacity to remember facts or experiences or both.

The Reminiscence Bump is the increased recollection by older adults of events that occurred during childhood, adolescence, and early adulthood (https://goo.gl/xd0PVF)

The term Autobiographical Memory arises in the work of Cohen and Conway:
- Williams, H. L., Conway, M. A., & Cohen, G. (2008). Autobiographical memory. In G. Cohen & M. A. Conway (Eds.), Memory in the Real World (3rd ed., pp. 21-90). Hove, UK: Psychology Press.
- Dorthe Bersten, The Unbidden Past, Involuntary Autobiographical Memorie, Arhus University, Current Directions in Psychological Science 2010 19: 138. (https://goo.gl/EkTTSP)

## Chapter 9: Kenya
- Sam Reifler, I Ching, The World's Oldest and Most Revered System of Fortune Telling, Bantum, 1974

## Chapter 10: Taboo

Citylit is a college in Covent Garden London which offers over a hundred writing courses every term and where many big names in literature have trained and taught. (https://goo.gl/JFBaxg)

On taboo-breaking in memoirs about fathers
- Andre Gerard, Top Ten Father Memoirs, The Guardian, 12 June 2013 (https://goo.gl/RTjqLO)
- Andre Gerard, Beyond Memoir and Biography, Edmund Gosse and the Patremoir, 17 July 2013 (https://goo.gl/vquDHM)
- Edmund Gosse, Father and Son, Heinemann, 1907

On the secrets of our best known and celebrated memoir writers:
- William Zinsser (Ed), Inventing The Truth - The Art and Craft of Memoir, Houghton Mifflin, 1998

On auto-ethnography:
- Ellis, C. (1991). Sociological Introspection and Emotional Experience. Symbolic Interaction, 14, 23-50.
- Ellis, C & Bochner, A (2000), Auto-ethnography, Personal Narrative, Reflexity: Research as Subject. In, N. Denszin & Y Lincoln (eds.), The Handbook of Qualitative Research (2nd ed.) (pp. 733-768). Thousand Oaks, CA. Sage

## Chapter 12: Fun (Dad #1)
- Jo Grimond MP, Liberal History (https://goo.gl/y7IyRq)
- History of Hildenburg Hall (https://goo.gl/hvv2yY)

Evangelism in the UK:
- Video of Billy Graham's Wembley Crusade 1955, YouTube (https://goo.gl/vyzLMO).
- John Capon, Sixty years on: Billy Graham's London Crusade, Church Times, posted 23 May 2014 (https://goo.gl/kLHQK1)
- Ian M Randall, Conservative Constructionist: The Early Influence of Billy Graham in Britain, Evangelical Quarterly 67:4 (1995), 309-333 (https://goo.gl/a0UwUM)

- Jean Rees, His Name Was Tom, The Biography of Tom Rees, Hodder and Stoughton, 1971
- On Hildenborough Hall from Hildenborough History Society (https://goo.gl/olFZYM)

## Chapter 13: Strict (Dad #2)

- Alex Proud, Was 1963 The Best Year To Be a Man? Daily Telegraph, 28 Nov 2013 (https://goo.gl/JTu1pw)
- Paul Feeney, A 1960s Childhood: From Thunderbirds to Beatlemania, The History Press, 2010
- John Robinson, Honest To God, Westminster John Knox Press, 1963
- Maidstone a Closer Look, A Review of Social Services, Maidstone and District Council of Churches, 1965

## Chapter 14: Crash

- USA Office of the Historian, The Cuban Missile Crisis, October 1962, (https://goo.gl/Qfu43t)
- JFK Library, The Cold War, (https://goo.gl/cPwjJI)
- The Macy Conferences 1941-1960 (https://goo.gl/UwxYVn)
- W Ross Ashby, An Introduction to Cybernetics, chapman and Hall, 1956
- Aldous Huxley, Ends and Means (An Inquiry into the Nature of Ideals and Into the Methods Employed for Their Realisation), Chatto & Windus, 1937

## Chapter 15: Hippie ( Dad #3) and the Hammer Blows

The Sixties creative explosion:

- You Say You Want a Revolution, Exhibition, V&A London, 2016 (https://goo.gl/gu7j9X)
- A Dizzying Trip to the Heart of the 1960s, Alexis Petridis, The Guardian, 7 Sep 2016, (https://goo.gl/u6l6zn)
- Was 1966 Pop's Best Year Ever? Sean O'Hagan, Ed Vulliamy and Barbara Ellen, The Guardian, 31 January 2016 (https://goo.gl/XJ27aU)

North-Western Polytechnic opened in 1929 in Kentish Town, London, specialising in social sciences, humanities and arts, became London's largest polytechnic in 1967.

## Chapter 16: Growth of The Movement
Setting inspired by:
- Simon Denny, Products for Organising, Serpentine Sackler Gallery, London, November 2015, (https://goo.gl/JY84D5)

On the early history of NTL:
- NTL Institute website: Over 67 Years at the Forefront of Experiential Learning, (https://goo.gl/cTGhtY) Accessed 1 Dec 2016

On Personal Development within Corporate America:
- Art Kleiner, The Age of Heretics, Jossey Bass, 2008

## Chapter 17: Secrets and Lies
- Carl R Rogers, On Becoming A Person, New Ed, Robinson, 2004

Therapy Session inspired by Fritz Perls in late 1960s on YouTube. Also:
- Frederick Perls, Ralph F. Hefferline, Paul Goodman, Gestalt Therapy: Excitement and Growth in Human Personality, Penguin, 1951

## Chapter 18: Gone (Dad #4)
The Ragged Trousered Philanthropists, an authentic story of working class life in Britain by an Irish painter decorator working in Hastings, was first published in 1914. This contribution is acknowledged by many in the British socialist movement.
- Robert Tressell, The Ragged Trousered Philanthropists, Harper, 2004

- Bob and Carol and Ted and Alice: a 1969 Comedy Drama film by Paul Mazursky, starting Natalie Wood and Elliot Gould (https://goo.gl/cLqowa)

Lighthouse Encounter Group run by tutor from Esalen:
- Will Schutz, The Human Element, Jossey Bass, 1994
- Esalen Memorial Tributes, Will Schutz, Accessed 1 Dec 2016 (https://goo.gl/NTRIoE)
- Carl R Rogers, Encounter Groups, Pelican, 1970
- Special Report on Encounter Group, Newsweek, 12

May 1969 (https://goo.gl/cE23G3)

## Chapter 19: Vienna

Sigmund Freud Museum at 19 Berggase in Vienna is open to the public (https://goo.gl/Xkzdn2)

- Freud and the Unconscious Mind (https://goo.gl/4rkWMT)
- Mark Vernon, 100 Years and Making a Comeback – Freud's Theories of the Unconscious, The Guardian, 30 November 2015 (https://goo.gl/rhKPlX)

The tabletop method used in Café Schwarzenberg borrows from Family Constellations by Bert Hellinger (https://goo.gl/7YCcpC).

Sonny Boy song (https://goo.gl/tHtkmE)

Jung's dream is in Robert A Johnson, Owning Your Own Shadow, Harper, 1991, p48.
For more on Shadow see:

- Daryl Sharp, Digesting Jung , Inner City Books, 2001 (https://goo.gl/4KLZQK)
- C G Jung, Memories, Dreams, Reflections, Fontana, 1995
- Connie Zweig and Jeremiah Abrams (Ed), Meeting The Shadow, Tarcher, 1990
- The Hidden Power of the Dark Side of Human Nature, Tarcher Putnam, 1991
- R L Stevenson, The Strange Case of Dr Jekyll and Mr Hyde, Longmans, Green and Co, 1886

On despatch riders in WW1:

- Motor Bike Times (https://goo.gl/OQdd1k)
- Austin Patrick Corcoran, The Daredevil of the British Army, Leonaur, 2011

On perfectionism

- Perfectionists Vulnerable To Depression, American Psychological Association, May 2006 (https://goo.gl/Y38vws)
- Dr Luisa Dillner, Should I Stop Being A Perfectionist? The Guardian, 20 April 2014 (https://goo.gl/IE12t8)

## Chapter 20: Surreal Adventure Reprise
- Alain Fournier, Le Grand Meaulnes, Paris, Emile Paul Frere, 1913

## Chapter 21: Misnomers
On warrior, dreamer, thinker, lover:
- Nate Boaz and Erica Ariel Fox, Change Leader, Change Thyself, McKinsey Quarterly, March 2014 (https://goo.gl/En6Ss7)

## Chapter 23: Wishful Thinking
- William Shakespeare, As You Like It - All the World's a Stage Speech, also known as The Seven Ages of Man, (https://goo.gl/aMWHZo)
- Arnold Van Gennep, Rites of Passage, University of Chicago Press, 1960 (https://goo.gl/lPMx8k)

## Chapter 24: Coming Back to Life
About Villa Lilly:
- Therapiedorf Villa Lilly (https://goo.gl/26q6D9)
- The Bitter Tale of the Budweiser Family (https://goo.gl/vkcHTG)
- Adolphus Busch (https://goo.gl/qLrO66)
- Wikipedia (https://goo.gl/a8Qr5V)
- Otto Muehl (https://goo.gl/qfZVQO)

There is recent evidence of widespread drug use in Hitler's Germany which challenges our understanding of the second world war:
- Norman Ohler, Blitzed, Penguin, 2017 (https://goo.gl/Yfq3d4)

Dad's reflections on parenting derived from Eric Berne's Transactional Analysis:
- Thomas A Harris, I'm OK- You're OK, Harper & Row, 1967

## Chapter 25: Closing the Box
- Ira Progoff, The Death and Rebirth of Psychology, McGraw Hill, 1956
- Ira Progoff, Jung's Psychology and Its Social Meaning, Routledge, New Ed, 1999
- Khalil Gibran, The Prophet, Alfred A Knopf, 1923

On paternal experiences and fatherly advice
- Ted Kessler, My Old Man – Tales of Our Fathers (https://goo.gl/03wYJT)
- Maria Popova, Letters of Fatherly Advice From History's Greatest Public Dads, Brainpickings (https://goo.gl/9vW8kJ)

## Appendix 1. On Becoming a Psychologist
- Tony Page, Diary of a Change Agent, Gower, 1996
- Philip Goodwin and Tony Page, Creating Leadership: How to Change Hippos into Gazelles, BEP, 2018

## Appendix 2. Storytelling as Therapy
On narrative therapy: (https://goo.gl/9htYpV)

## Appendix 3. An Unofficial Story of the "Cult of Self" and What's Coming Next
For Hunter-gatherers and agricultural revolution, see Wikipedia: https://goo.gl/P4TmjZ

E H Gombrich, A Little History of the World, DuMont, Cologne, 1985
Adam Smith quote: https://goo.gl/7rXZP2
Altruism and Auguste Comte: https://goo.gl/F1i3pd

On Narcissism:
- The History of Narcissism including Freud's famous paper of 1914 (https://goo.gl/JeFuSl)
- Zoe Williams, Me! Me! Me! Are we living through a Narcissism Epidemic? The Guardian, 2 March 2016 (https://goo.gl/tcqA1E)
- Michael Maccoby, Nacissistic Leaders, Harvard Business Review, Jan 2004
- Mark Vernon, Viewpoint: In Defence of Narcissism, BBC News Magazine, 10 October 2012 (https://goo.gl/dmkBmP)
- Christian Jarrett, There's Such a Thing as Collective Narcissism (and it might explain a lot that's going on at the moment), BPS Research Digest, 9 December 2016 (https://goo.gl/wIPAqU)
- Deborah Orr, I Grew Up In A Man's World. I Know the Damage Narcissistic Men Can Do. The Guardian, 27

January 2017

A controversy surrounding spontaneous remission from mental illness:

- H J Eysenck, The Effects of Psychotherapy: An Evaluation, Journal of Consulting Psychology, 16(5), 319-324. 1952
- H J Eysenck, A Unified Theory of Psychotherapy, Behaviour Therapy and Spontaneous Remission, Zeitschrift für Psychologie mit Zeitschrift für angewandte Psychologie, 188(1), 43-56, 1980
- Michael J Lambert, Spontaneous Remission in Adult Neurotic Disorders: A Revision and summary, Psychological Bulletin, 1976

Universal Declaration of Human Rights: https://goo.gl/QgwmHk

- On Humanistic Psychology, Association of Humanistic Psychology, Human Potential Movement …
- Early innovators: https://goo.gl/kSZQMd
- Human Potential Movement: https://goo.gl/5XC96K
- Preliminary meetings: https://goo.gl/gGkrKj
- Aldous Huxley: https://goo.gl/igGLhL
- Abraham H Maslow, Towards a Psychology of Being, D Van Norstrand, 1968
- Three forces of psychology: Jeffrey J. Kripal, Esalen: America and the Religion of No Religion, Chicago, 2007
- AHP's growth in Britain from 1969: John Rowan, Ordinary Ecstasy The Dialectics of Humanistic Psychology, Chapter 12: The Spread of Humanistic Psychology, Routledge, 2015 (https://goo.gl/hcr1vu)
- Europe vs America: Roger Harrison, Letter From London, AHP Newsletter Summer 1972 (https://goo.gl/j5ZTG0)
- Leni Wildflower, The Hidden History of Coaching, Open University Press, 2013
- Andrew Bland and Eugene DeRoberts, Maslow's Unacknowledged Contributions to Developmental Psychology, Journal of Humanistic Psychology, 2017

Anti-psychiatry: https://goo.gl/TEq4Sx

A widely used manual for the classification of mental illness is 'DSM-5', the Diagnostic and Statistical Manual of Mental Disorders, Fifth Edition (https://goo.gl/nXVM2p)

On the proposal that a personality disorder is heritable:
- Martin Brune, Borderline Personality Disorder: Why 'fast and furious'? Evol Med Public Health (2016) 2016 (1): 52-66 (https://goo.gl/Qwv0NX)

## Appendix 4. When Rebirthing Is Wishful Thinking and When It Isn't

Inspirations for the rebirthing scene included:
- The Two Ronnies, Arcola Theatre, Dalston 2015
- R D Laing, Knots, Tavistock, 1970
- On Laing by Thomas Szasz: https://goo.gl/yBxe69
- Laing and authenticity: https://goo.gl/uBxU99
- Laing's career timeline: https://goo.gl/KQkZre
- Laing, healing and shamanism: https://goo.gl/ATi9oJ
- Characteristics of rebirthing sessions: https://goo.gl/Ydu9nA
- According to Laing's son Adrian: https://goo.gl/qSZUDX
- Influence of Elizabeth Fehr: https://goo.gl/HmHehT
- On Laing's meeting Elizabeth Fehr: https://goo.gl/LtUnFa

Laing's only encounter with Rogers in 1978
On the explosive night before: https://goo.gl/wVxzw6, https://goo.gl/qZqQPd
On the public debate in the London Hilton: https://goo.gl/S8H62F
By Daniel Burston: https://goo.gl/Ydu9nA
By Eduardo Bandeira: https://goo.gl/Tvuyuw

## Appendix 5. Placing Ourselves in System and Society - Five Principles

The method of Family Constellations by Bert Hellinger:
- John Whittington, Systemic Coaching And Constellations, Kogan Page, 2012
- Jan Jacob Stam, Fields of Connection, Bert Hellinger Instituut, Netherlands, 2010 (https://goo.gl/qrNMXJ)
- For Burt Hellinger see Wikipedia https://goo.gl/oodvRE

For Villa Lilly see Chapter 24.

On Reciprocity:
- For developing gratitude, modesty and compassion see https://goo.gl/ru8ayQ, https://goo.gl/tcqA1E
- Tony Page, Sustaining Reciprocity in an Era of Narcissism… or bringing it back to 'us', e-Organisations and People, Summer 2017.

Much of Appendix 5 and the three final questions were inspired by Sarah Henrey's session on Somatic coaching and Constellations that took place at Sadler Heath in Lewes, under the facilitation of Pattie Horrocks in September 2017.

# Acknowledgements

To all those who have shared their father stories with me, or contributed in so far unacknowledged ways to what is written here.

The Learning Set for giving space to our fathers, and for encouraging me to keep going with this.

David Webster for going off-piste into this personal "family and father" theme, making it safe to take off my professional hat during our supervision sessions.

The ferryman at Bawdsey for getting us safely to the other side.

Michael Schwind, the patients and staff of Therapiedorf Villa Lilly for a timely reminder about what a difference belief makes.

The writers. Professor Bob McKenzie and all those he gathers in the AMED Writers' Group for encouraging us to practice together and enjoy the art of writing. Neil Arksey and the creative writing class at City Lit. Steve Dilworth for showing me that this kind of writing has a name: auto-ethnography.

The readers. Mary Joyce, Jeremy Keeley, Gordon Lyle and Tritia Neeb from whose feedback as "first readers", given with such care, came the courage to speak with my own voice. Ella and The Ella Mesma Company for checking and improving the dance of rebirthing in Appendix 4. Cousin K and Helen for reading the final draft. And once again the writing class at City Lit.

Ian Florance for sparking my interest in the Bad Boys and Girls of the Human Potential Movement, for the interview in Psychologist Magazine, all his wisdom and generous guidance on the path to publication.

Philip Mann whose experience as a former Art Director at Secker & Warburg, William Heinemann, and Macmillan Publishers contributed to this special cover design and layout, not to mention his special viewpoint as an olive farmer and trench digger in the Cretan hills.

The family. Auntie M and Uncle D for answering my nagging questions when others dodged them, and for giving such generous support to the wider family.

Uncle R and Cousins C, B, K, K, M, S, V and W, for your recollections.

The Boys for being The Boys. To our Grandpa and Grandma, Mum and Dad, and of course our sister.

Helen, Wilson and Nancy not only for your encouragement with this, but for being family, and for being with me before, during and after the quest.

And anyone I've missed.

Made in the USA
Columbia, SC
25 February 2018